A GRACIOUS PLENTY

RECIPES AND STORIES FROM

THE DODGE HILL INN

A GRACIOUS PLENTY

RECIPES AND STORIES FROM

THE DODGE HILL INN

by

ANN HEMPERLEY DOBBS

&

HELEN HARDIN PETERSON

Copyright © 2014
Ann Hemperley Dobbs and Helen Hardin Peterson
Editor: Terri Peterson LaFavor

Front Cover Watercolor of the Dodge Hill Inn, Eastman, Georgia,
Painted by Laura Leigh McCook Kirkley and used by permission.

All rights reserved. Copyright under Berne Copyright Convention, and Pan-American Copyright Convention. No part of this book may be reproduced, stored in a retrieval system, or transmitted in any form, or by any means: electronic, mechanical, photocopying, recording, or otherwise, without prior permission of the author.

ISBN: 978-0-9892491-95 (Trade paperback)

Published by MM John Welda BookHouse
P.O. Box 111, Eastman, Georgia 31023

For more information on this book and the authors:
http://www.lightwood.com

~Dedication~

As always, Helen and I would like to dedicate this cookbook to the memory of our mothers, who gave us the connection to a great family and to each other.

Willilu Burch Hemperley　　**Evelyn Burch Hardin**
Ann's mother　　*Helen's mother*

Helen Hardin Peterson   Ann Hemperley Dobbs

~Acknowledgements~

Helen and I deeply appreciate the culinary heritage left to us by our mothers and our grandmother, Eva Roebuck Burch. We would also like to acknowledge our dependence upon my mother's cookbook, *Recipes of a Georgia Burch Gal*, which she published in 1993. For technical advice in the first edition of *A Gracious Plenty*, we consulted our cousin Eve McCranie Jones and her husband Phil. For expert advice in compiling this edition, we turned to Terri Peterson LaFavor, who served faithfully and long as the editor of this volume. Her technical expertise made it possible for us to produce a superior cookbook in the form of this final edition. We could never have done it without Cousin Terri.

Most of all, we wish to acknowledge the blessing of a host of cousins. We are thankful to have one for every need. Not a one of them, however, reads and studies as many cook books as Cousin Helen. Helen peruses magazines and cook books and tunes in to the Food Network, and she is intrepid in trying out tempting new recipes. She never rests on her laurels. Don't hesitate to follow her lead, and try some of these new recipes. Helen Peterson has become famous in this community for her cakes and pies, which she often bakes for her friends and neighbors. Of course, there are many wonderfully inspired cooks in Eastman; but it is quite likely that Helen Peterson is the *best cook in town*. If I were a betting woman, I'd put money on it!

~Ann Dobbs

Foreword

My cousin Helen Peterson and I have been occasional companions in the kitchen for as long as I can remember. Although I lived in Fulton County and she lived in Dodge, we shared many summers together. We were the first and foremost mud pie makers in the county, even before we went to school. Furthermore, we were talented in transforming chinaberry "peas" into succulent vegetables with irresistible sauces.

Our first alfresco kitchen had board-and-brick tables and a play stove made from brick and old pipe. Our "house," always hospitable, was defined by sticks and rocks, laid out in a square on the ground. That was all the definition we needed; the walls and roof rose in our imaginations. We had "children," of course—as many little ones as the dolls we had collected. They added joy to our days, and rode about languidly in wagons and baby carriages.

If it rained, we retreated from the side yard to Aunt Evelyn's front porch, where Helen assembled her house at one end, and I assembled mine at the other. We visited, set a tea table at her place and then at mine, and gossiped in girlish whispers. When we tired of this activity, we created miniature rooms from old Sears & Roebuck catalogues, just as our mothers had done before us. We always included a fine kitchen with all the latest appliances.

We sometimes got in a bit of fishing; we liked nothing better than catching red-eyes in a nearby creek. After one successful fishing expedition, Aunt Evelyn set our tea table on the back porch, fried up our string of fresh fish, and left us to our feast.

These were the magical summers of our childhood. Neither Helen nor I dreamed that we were destined to "play house" again when we both retired. Now we share Inn duties and kitchen responsibilities at The Dodge Hill Inn. Maybe that is the best of all!

~Ann Dobbs

Contents

Dedication, Foreword, and Acknowledgements

Breakfast — 1

Party Foods — 23

Sandwiches — 41

Breads and Pastries — 49

Salads — 63

Soups, Casseroles, and Main Dishes — 79

Vegetable Dishes — 97

Cakes, Pies, and Desserts — 105

Church Dinners — 141

The "Amen" — 155

Post Script (P.S.) — 157

About the Authors — 159

Index — 161

A GRACIOUS PLENTY

RECIPES AND STORIES FROM
THE DODGE HILL INN

This cookbook was compiled by two Southern ladies who place little confidence in fad diets. Instead, we have confidence in the wholesome foods favored by our maternal ancestors, and we have never lost our faith in the egg.

Breakfast

"We had our breakfast—whatever happens in a house, robbery or murder, it doesn't matter, you must have your breakfast."
　　　　The wise words of Gabriel Betteredge, the butler, in *The Moonstone*, by Wilkie Collins

In 1868, when Wilkie Collins wrote the world's first detective novel, it was unthinkable for an Englishman to miss his breakfast. The night-long fast *must* be broken. Sherlock Holmes and Dr. Watson, for all the weighty matters they pondered, were diligent in partaking of this meal. Today, many people with far fewer concerns and enigmas than Doyle could devise are unacquainted with the pleasure of sitting down to breakfast.

At one time, every new house plan had a breakfast room. I haven't seen a breakfast room in years! And yet, to turn over in bed, to look out the window at a brightening sky, and to smell the aroma of breakfast cooking—these things are the most innocent and pleasurable of sensory experiences.

Helen and I always loved breakfast and always prepared this meal for our own husbands and our children when they were young and living at home. On the occasions when we brought our children to visit their cousins, a new generation snuggled among the covers, sniffed the bacon cooking, and anticipated pleasures to come.

Today, at our Bed and Breakfast Inn, we take great pleasure in cooking and serving the first meal of the day to our guests. Many people say, "I don't eat breakfast." What they really mean, we have discovered, is that they don't *cook* breakfast, and no one cooks it for them. A sausage biscuit with a cup of coffee from McDonald's is as near as they come to a breakfast experience.

Eating breakfast intensifies the joys of the morning, and reminds us that the chill of fresh juice and the warmth of fragrant coffee—taken at leisure—is its very best beginning. The following recipes should keep your breakfast guests delighted, from the first sip to the last crunch. Thus, until the breakfast room returns, we will do what we can to keep breakfast alive.

Breakfast Recipes from The Dodge Hill Inn

When we have guests at The Dodge Hill Inn, we try to serve them something different for breakfast every morning. Everyone we serve seems to enjoy our pancakes and waffles. The recipes below are those we use at the Inn, and they are the best waffle and pancake recipes we have ever found.

Waffles

4 eggs, separated	2 cups milk
3 cups self-rising flour (White Lily)	1 T sugar (optional)
(If using plain flour, add 3 t baking powder and 1 t salt)	
1/2 cup liquid shortening (Wesson Oil)	

Beat egg whites. Beat yolks with oil, add milk, then add dry ingredients (flour and sugar), blending with a whisk just until liquid is absorbed. Fold in whites. Bake in preheated, hot waffle iron. Follow manufacturer's directions.

Pancakes

1 1/2 cups self rising flour	1 or 2 eggs, separated
3 T sugar	3 T oil
½ cup sweet milk, ½ cup buttermilk	

<u>For a Crowd</u>

3 cups self rising flour	2 or 3 eggs, separated
6 T sugar	6 T oil
1 cup sweet milk, 1 cup buttermilk	

Sift flour together with sugar into a bowl. In separate bowl, beat egg whites. In third bowl, beat yolks, add oil, and beat together. To yolk mixture, add milk and blend. Stir liquids into flour mixture. Fold in whites. Bake on hot griddle turning once.

French Toast Puff

2 cups self-rising flour	1 ½ cups milk
2 T sugar	1 T vanilla
2 eggs	1 sliced loaf French bread

Sift flour and sugar together into large bowl. In a second bowl, beat eggs, and add milk and vanilla. Add to flour mixture and blend well. In an electric skillet, heat cooking oil to 350°. Dip the bread in the batter, coating well and evenly. Cook until golden on both sides, and drain on paper towels. Sprinkle with 10X powdered sugar and serve with maple syrup.

Everybody needs to know how to make . . .

A Pan of Hot Biscuits

Helen always makes buttermilk biscuits, and they are always delicious: high, puffy, and soft. If you wish, make them ahead, bake them to a light brown, cover, and reheat when ready to serve. They will be perfect. Sweet milk biscuits are crustier, but my dad and brother always wanted their biscuits very thin, in the form of "two crusts." (My husband Don was happy to have either variety.) Actually, both varieties are excellent!

Biscuits

2 cups sifted self-rising flour (White Lily)   4-5 T Crisco shortening
3/4 cup sweet milk or 4/5 cup buttermilk

Sift the flour, measure, and sift again into a mixing bowl. Cut in the shortening with a pastry blender, working from the outside of the bowl toward the center, turning the bowl as you work. Add the milk. Add a dab more if dough is too dry.

Flour hands well, lift the dough, and place on a pastry cloth. Add a dab more flour if necessary. Knead the dough a few turns, lifting it with the fingers and pushing it forward with the heel of the hand. Roll out to about ¼ inch thickness. Cut biscuits with a cutter, place on baking sheet, and bake at 450° until done.

Cinnamon Biscuits

Make biscuit dough as directed above. Roll into rectangle. Melt 1/3 stick butter in small sauce pan or in Pyrex dish in microwave. In small bowl, combine 1/3 cup granulated sugar and 1 t cinnamon. Spread melted butter over dough. Sprinkle sugar mixture over dough and roll from long side to opposite edge. When you have a long roll, cut across it to make individual biscuit swirls. Place each swirled biscuit on greased cookie sheet, cut side down. Bake at 425° until done, about eight minutes.

Place 1 cup powdered sugar in mixing bowl. Add 2 T half and half. Beat with hand mixer until creamy. Add 1 T vanilla. Spread on hot cinnamon biscuits.

Egg Tortillas

6 large flour tortillas   2 green onions, chopped
6 scrambled eggs   1 ½ cups cheddar cheese
Salt and pepper to taste   Sour cream and salsa

Scramble eggs with salt and pepper and spread down the center of each tortilla. Sprinkle with onions (or chives) and grated cheese. Roll up. Cut in half diagonally and place in greased baking dish. Top with additional cheese and sprinkle with paprika. Broil until cheese is bubbly. Serve with sour cream and salsa, if desired.

Tomato and Basil Frittata

8 oz sharp cheddar cheese	½ cup half and half
1 T flour or ground oatmeal	1 T Worcestershire sauce
4 oz Monterey Jack cheese	1 medium tomato, chopped
6 eggs beaten	¼ cup fresh basil or chives

Grate cheddar cheese and toss with flour. Place in greased pie plate. Sprinkle grated Monterey Jack cheese over top. In a separate mixing bowl, beat eggs and pour in half and half. Add Worcestershire sauce. Mix well and pour over cheeses. Sprinkle chopped tomato and chopped herbs over egg and cheese. Refrigerate overnight, if desired. Bake in 350º oven for 30 to 35 minutes.

Caramel French Toast

1 cup brown sugar	5 eggs
½ cup butter	1 ½ cups milk
2 T light corn syrup	1 T vanilla extract
1 loaf French bread, in ¾ inch slices	¼ cup sugar, 1 t cinnamon

In medium sauce pan, over medium low heat, mix and melt brown sugar, butter, and corn syrup. Meanwhile, spray a 9 X 13 baking dish with Pam. Pour butter and sugar mixture into baking dish. Arrange bread slices over this syrup. Whisk together eggs, milk, and vanilla. Pour over bread slices, not missing any areas, and using all the mixture. The bread slices will absorb excess. Sprinkle cinnamon sugar mixture over all. Cover the baking dish and refrigerate overnight. Bake uncovered in 350º oven for 30 to 45 minutes. Serve directly from baking dish, inverting slices onto plate.

Favorite Breakfast Casserole

6 slices white loaf bread	2 cups milk
1 ½ cups grated cheese	Pinch of salt
6 eggs	Pepper to taste

If desired, trim the crusts from the bread. Cube each slice, using electric knife. Place bread cubes in greased 8 x12 Pyrex baking dish. Sprinkle grated cheese over the bread slices. If you wish, a pound of sausage, well browned and drained, or a cup of cooked, chopped ham, may be added over bread and before adding cheese. Beat eggs, add milk and beat again, and pour over all. Cover and refrigerate overnight. This soufflé bakes beautifully in a water bath. Try it! Fill a 10 x 16 baking dish with about an inch of water, and place the filled casserole into it and it will cook to perfection. Bake the casserole for about 30 minutes at 350º. Be very careful when removing casserole from the oven!

Crepes

Guests at the Inn so often call us "Miss Ann" and "Miss Helen," that we tend to address each other in the same way. We are almost always polite to each other in the kitchen. However, there are limits: Miss Helen does not allow Miss Ann to make crepes, as Helen is the neatest and best crepe maker in town and does not enjoy seeing a mess in the kitchen. Here's her secret recipe! If you use it, be neat. (Helen advises against a crepe-maker that must be turned upside down to dip into the batter.)

Crepes

1 cup all purpose flour
¼ t salt
1¼ cups milk

2 large eggs
2 T melted butter

Place everything in blender except butter. Blend, slowly adding the melted butter. Chill one hour. Coat the bottom of non-stick 8-inch frying pan with Pam. Heat to medium high. Pour 2 T batter into pan and quickly tilt pan in all directions, covering the bottom surface. Cook one minute, or until crepes can be shaken loose. Turn over and cook 30 seconds. Dump out on a cloth towel to cool. Crepes may be frozen with waxed paper between and used as needed.

When you are ready to serve crepes, lightly grease a baking pan and place crepes on the surface. Add a scoop of scrambled eggs, fresh from the skillet. Over these, pour some cream sauce. Roll up each crepe, placing seam side down, and sprinkle with grated cheese and paprika. Place under broiler until bubbling. In a serving plate, pour a tablespoon or two of the cream sauce, making a nest for the crepe. Lift the crepe carefully on to the cream sauce, using a wide pancake turner. Add more sauce around the edges. Garnish with a few sprigs of parsley.

An excellent cream sauce:

In saucepan, melt 2 T butter over medium heat. Add 2 T self-rising flour. Mix and cook until thick. Gradually add 2 cups milk, and stir until you have a creamy sauce. Use in above recipe, or serve on vegetables.

Blueberry Muffins

1 cup blueberries, fresh or frozen
¾ cup sugar
1 3/4 cups self-rising flour

1/4 cup Wesson oil
1 egg
½ cup milk

Wash fresh blueberries and drain on paper towels, or rinse frozen blueberries and drain. Mix flour with sugar and sift together into bowl. Add oil, unbeaten egg, and milk, and beat until smooth. Stir in drained blueberries. Spoon into greased muffin pans. Bake at 350° for 20-25 minutes. Makes 12-14 muffins.

This recipe makes delicious, fragrant, and crusty muffins. If you have no blueberries, just make plain ones. Both are wonderful.

Apple Sauce Muffins

<u>Cream together</u>—
    2 sticks softened margarine or butter
    2 cups sugar
    2 eggs
    1 t vanilla

<u>Sift together and add to above</u>—
    4 cups plain flour
    3 t cinnamon
    1 t cloves
    2 t allspice

<u>Stir together and add to blended mixture</u>—
    2 t baking soda
    1-16 oz can of apple sauce

<u>Add</u>— 1 cup chopped pecans.

Fill muffin cups 1/2 full and bake at 350° for 20 minutes. Batter will keep a week in refrigerator and can be used as needed.

Orange Biscuits

4 T butter	3 t baking powder (with plain flour)
1 t grated orange rind	1 t salt (with plain flour)
½ cup sugar	¼ cup shortening
1 T hot water	Juice of one orange
2 cups sifted flour (plain) or	Milk to increase liquid to 2/3 cup
2 cups self-rising flour	

Melt 2 T of the butter in a 9-inch round pan. Blend grated orange rind and sugar. Add ¼ cup of the orange/sugar mixture to melted butter in the pan. Add the 1 tablespoon water to remaining orange/sugar. Set aside. Sift together flour, baking powder, and salt. (If self-rising flour is used, omit baking powder and salt.) Cut in shortening. Add juice of one orange and milk to make a soft dough. Turn out on floured board and knead for 30 seconds.

Roll dough into a 10-12 inch rectangle, ¼ inch thick. Melt remaining butter and brush over the top of the dough. Sprinkle remaining orange and sugar mixture over all. Roll up like jelly roll. Cut in 12 portions. Place cut side down on top of sugar mixture in pan. Bake in an oven 450° until browned, about 15 minutes. Remove from pan and serve. Makes 12 biscuits.

Ham and Eggs a la Swiss

6 English muffins	¾ cup sour cream
6 boiled eggs	¾ cup mayonnaise
12 ham slices	1 ½ cups Swiss cheese

Split muffins. Butter each muffin half and toast on baking sheet until lightly browned. Place slices of ham on each half. You may use pre-cooked ham or slices of home baked ham. Place sliced boiled eggs on top of ham slices. Mix mayonnaise and sour cream. Spread over eggs. Cover with cheese and sprinkle with paprika. Broil until bubbly and slightly browned on top.

Quiche

1 small, chopped onion	½ t salt and ¼ t pepper
1 T bacon fat	2 ½ cups grated Swiss cheese
3 eggs	6 slices bacon, cooked crisp,
½ cup sour cream, ½ cup half and half	drained, and crumbled

Cook onion in bacon fat just until tender. Set aside. Beat eggs, sour cream, half and half, and seasonings. Then stir in onion, grated cheese, and crumbled bacon. Pour into unbaked pie shell and bake at 375º for 30 minutes or until custard is set. For crust, see bread section.

Cheese Soufflé

3 T butter	¾ t dry mustard
4 T flour	1 ½ t sugar
¼ t salt	2 t water
1 cup milk	3 eggs, separated
1 cup grated, sharp cheddar cheese	

In a sauce pan, melt butter over medium heat. Stir in the flour and salt. Slowly add the milk, whisking to make a sauce. Add cheese and stir until melted. In a small bowl, mix mustard and sugar in water. Add to sauce. Add egg yolks and beat in well. In a separate bowl, beat egg whites until peaks form. Fold into sauce. Pour in greased individual Pyrex custard cups, one for each person. Place cups in a baking pan containing an inch and a half of water. Bake at 350º for 15-20 minutes, until puffed and slightly browned. Serve immediately.

Scrambled Eggs

Break 2 to 6 eggs in a bowl and add 1 T milk for each egg. Beat eggs with wire whisk until very light. Pour into a heated iron skillet or non-stick frying pan, well buttered, and stir continually until perfectly scrambled.

Grits

Place 3 cups water in heavy sauce pan
Add 1 cup quick or regular grits and 1 t salt to cold water
Add 3 T butter
When thickened, add 1 cup of milk

Stir this mixture over high heat until water boils. After water and grits come to a boil, lower heat. Continue to stir often as the grits bubble along. As the mixture begins to thicken, add a cup of milk. Stir until blended, turn burner to low, and cover. Allow the grits to continue to cook until you are ready to serve. Add more milk if necessary.

Grits Casserole

Use recipe above, but remove from the stove when grits thicken and before adding milk. Add four beaten eggs, two cups milk rather than one, a half pound of grated cheddar cheese, and stir until blended. Pour into greased baking pan. Bake at 350° until set.

Parmesan Potatoes

6 medium size potatoes	1 t salt
½ cup grated parmesan cheese	1 t pepper
¼ cup flour, plain	4 T butter

Preheat oven to 350°. Peel the potatoes and cut into medium cubes. Place the cheese, flour, salt, and pepper into a plastic bag. Place potatoes in the bag and shake. Put butter into 9 X 13 inch pan, and place in heated oven just until butter melts. Remove the pan, and add the cubed potatoes. Toss. Bake at 350° for 20 minutes. Turn with spatula, and bake another 20 minutes, or until lightly browned and done. Serve hot with scrambled eggs.

Hot Spiced Fruit

1 # 2 can of sliced pineapple	1 cup juice from fruit
1 can pears	1 stick butter
1 can peaches	½ cup sugar
1 can apricots	2 T flour
1 jar maraschino cherries	1 t cinnamon, ½ t nutmeg

In a 9 X 13 inch casserole, arrange drained fruit. Melt butter in sauce pan. In separate bowl, mix the sugar and spices with the flour, and add the cup of fruit juice, blending until there are no lumps. Add sweetened juice to butter in pan and stir. Cook until thick. Pour over fruit. Cover and refrigerate overnight.

The next morning, bake uncovered at 350° for 45 minutes. Serve from the buffet in the baking dish.

Fried Apples

½ cup butter
6 apples, unpeeled, sliced, and cored
½ cup sugar

¾ t cinnamon
¼ cup sugar

Melt the stick of butter in a large, deep pan. Add the apples. Sprinkle with the ½ cup of sugar. Cover and cook about 15 minutes. Uncover, and add the cinnamon mixed with the ¼ cup of sugar. Cover and cook just until tender. This is a delicious breakfast fruit! If rushed, use a can of Luck's sliced apples.

Baked Apples

4 Granny Smith apples
4 T butter
4 T Georgia cane syrup

1 t cinnamon
1 t grated orange zest
4 T brown sugar

Spray baking pan with Pam. Preheat oven to 350°. Core apples and arrange in baking pan. There should be a hole in the middle of each apple. In small saucepan, melt butter and add syrup, cinnamon, orange rind, and sugar. When this mixture bubbles gently, pour it over the apples. Bake for 45 minutes.

Fresh Fruit

Use a combination of fruits in season: sliced peaches, strawberries, grapes, kiwi, oranges, and bananas, in any combination, are welcome and wonderful. If fresh peaches are available, one needs nothing else. In Middle Georgia, all these fruits (except bananas) are grown locally and may be combined pleasingly to satisfy a breakfast appetite. In local fields and orchards, strawberries are ripe first, followed by plums and peaches.

Fruit Bowl

Pour ½ cup orange juice into mixing bowl. (If strawberries are not sweet, add about ¼ cup sugar.) Cut a large variety of fruit into the bowl; stir. Dip into individual bowls with slotted spoon. To gild the lily, spoon chilled boiled custard over top. (See recipe below.)

Boiled Custard

4 cups whole milk	4 eggs
1 cup sugar, mixed with 1 scant T flour	1 t vanilla

Scald milk in top of a double boiler. In small bowl, mix flour and sugar. In another bowl, beat eggs thoroughly, and then add the combined dry ingredients. When milk is scalded (do not boil), pour a bit of the hot milk into a bowl containing the sugar and egg mixture. Stir. Return this mixture to the hot milk, stirring as you pour in. Stir continuously until the mixture will coat the spoon. Pour through a strainer into a large bowl. Add the vanilla. Allow to cool; custard will thicken as it cools. Refrigerate. The custard will be ready to top the fruit bowls in the morning, if it lasts that long.

Cream Cheese Danish

2 cans crescent rolls (8 count)
2-8oz packages cream cheese, softened
1 cup sugar

1 t vanilla
1 egg, separated
1 T sugar

Spray a 9 X 2 X 13 baking dish with Pam. Open one can of rolls, and spread the triangles out on the bottom of the dish, pinching seams together. Beat together the softened cream cheese, vanilla, 1 cup sugar, and egg yolk. Pour over the rolls, spreading to edge. Top with the other can of crescent rolls. Beat egg white until frothy, but still moist. Spread this liquid/frothy mix over the rolls. Sprinkle with 1 tablespoon sugar. Bake for 25-30 minutes at 350º.

Butterscotch Rolls

1 pack Rich's frozen roll dough
1 small package butterscotch pudding, not instant
1 stick butter

½ cup brown sugar
1/3 cup white sugar
1 t cinnamon

Grease generously a bundt pan, and fill with the individual rolls. Sprinkle with the dry pudding mix. Melt one stick of butter, add the sugars and cinnamon, and pour over the rolls. Cover with wax paper and leave at room temperature overnight. Bake 30 minutes at 350º. If it rises and starts to brown, lay a sheet of foil gently over top until done. Turn on to plate and serve at once.

Coffee Crumb Cake

This recipe is a grand solution to the challenge of a really big breakfast. The large recipe will serve 20 or more.

Large Recipe	Small Recipe
4 ½ cups self rising flour	2 ¼ cups self-rising flour
3 cups sugar	1 ½ cups sugar
¾ cup Crisco	1/3 cup Crisco
1 T cinnamon	1 ½ t cinnamon
4 eggs	2 eggs
1½ cups milk	¾ cup milk
1 t vanilla	½ t vanilla

Blend flour, sugar, and Crisco in electric mixer. Reserve 1¼ cups of this mixture. (For the small recipe, reserve 2/3 cup.) To this reserved mixture, add cinnamon and set aside.

To remaining dry mixture in mixing bowl, add eggs, milk, and vanilla. Beat in mixer at medium speed until batter is smooth and thickened. Pour batter into greased and floured baking pan. The large recipe requires one restaurant-sized pan, or two 9 x 13 Pyrex baking dishes. The small recipe will require one 9 X 13 pan. Sprinkle dry cinnamon-sugar mixture over top of raw batter in pan. Bake at 350° for 30 minutes, until cake is done. Check for doneness by touching cake lightly in the middle. If the dough springs back, the cake is done.

Apricot Coffee Cake

Grease well and flour a tube or bundt pan. Preheat oven to 350°.

1 cup butter	2 cups plain flour
2 cups sugar	1 t baking powder
2 eggs	¼ t salt
1 cup sour cream	1 cup slivered almonds
1 t almond extract	1-10 oz jar apricot preserves

Cream sugar and butter. Add eggs. Fold in cream and extract. Sift dry ingredients together and fold in. Put 1/3 of batter in pan. Top with half of the nuts and preserves. Pour in 1/3 more of the batter and top with remaining nuts and apricots. Add the last third, and bake at 350° for about 45 minutes.

This is a delicious cake, but it is a trick to get it out of the pan in one piece!

King and Prince Oatmeal Raisin Muffins

1 ¼ cup rolled oats	1 cup flour
1 ¼ cups buttermilk	1 ¼ t baking powder
2 eggs	½ t salt
¾ cup brown sugar	½ t baking soda
½ cup butter, melted and cooled	½ cup raisins

Combine the rolled oats and buttermilk in mixing bowl and let stand for 1 hour. Add the eggs, sugar, and butter. Mix 30 seconds. Scrape down bowl. Add combined dry ingredients and raisins. Mix on low speed about 15 seconds until dry ingredients are moistened. Fill sprayed muffin tins ½ full. Bake at 400° for 15-20 minutes. Yield: 1 dozen muffins.

These delicious muffins can't be beat! The King and Prince gave us their recipe.

Apple Dumplings

1 tube crescent rolls
2 Granny Smith apples
¾ cup butter
¾ cup orange juice
1 cup sugar

Peel and core apples. Cut into quarters. Wrap each quarter in 1 triangle of crescent dough. Place in greased baking dish. Cook orange juice and sugar until dissolved. Pour over dumplings and bake at 350° for 30 minutes.

Breakfast Cup

1/3 cup milk
1 egg
1 slice bread, cubed
Shredded cheddar cheese

Place bread in bottom of greased, individual ramekin. Beat egg; add milk, salt, and pepper. Pour over bread. Sprinkle with cheese. Place ramekins in baking pan containing one or two inches of water. Bake at 350° until set.

Fried Potato Patties

1½ cups mashed potatoes
2 eggs, beaten
Salt and pepper, to taste
½ cup self-rising flour
1 T chives, optional
Vegetable oil

Mix all ingredients except oil. Drop by rounded tablespoons into shallow oil heated to 350°. Fry on each side until lightly browned. Drain on paper towels. Serve with scrambled or fried eggs for breakfast. This is a terrific way to use leftover mashed potatoes.

Cranberry Banana Frappe

2 cups all-berry cranberry juice
1 cup fresh squeezed orange juice
¼ cup heavy whipping cream
1 T lemon juice

1 tray ice cubes (apple juice)
2 bananas
Fresh mint leaves
Fruit for garnish

Combine all ingredients except mint leaves in a blender. Process on high for one minute. Pour out and serve in crystal glasses or stemmed wine glasses. Garnish with fresh mint leaves and/or fruit.

Chilled Herbal Cooler

Red Zinger is the best of the herbal teas because of its zest, color, and flavor. Made by Celestial Seasonings, it is easy to find and simple to prepare.

8 Red Zinger Tea Bags
1 quart boiling water
1-12-ounce can frozen apple juice concentrate
4½ cups cold water
Ice cubes made from apple juice

¼ cup sugar
1 orange, sliced
1 lemon, sliced
Sprigs of mint

Place the tea bags in the boiling water, remove from heat, and allow to steep for at least 10-15 minutes. Remove bags and add all other ingredients except ice, fruit slices, and mint. Chill. When ready to serve, fill tall, crystal glasses with the ice cubes made from apple juice. Pour in the chilled tea and garnish with an orange slice, a lemon slice, and a sprig of mint.

At the breakfast table in summer, on a porch, or in a sunny dining room, "Chilled Herbal Cooler" is a refreshing change.

Slush

"Slush" is the favorite breakfast drink at The Dodge Hill Inn. Served ice cold, this drink is thick, delicious, and refreshing.

6 ripe bananas	3 cups water
1-6 oz can frozen lemonade	2 cups sugar
1-12 oz can frozen orange juice	2-28 oz bottles ginger ale
1-46 oz can pineapple juice	

Blend together all ingredients except ginger ale. Freeze. In the morning, thaw to a slush. Add ginger ale and serve. You may need to smooth ingredients in a blender or food processor again after they have been frozen.

We always double this recipe so that it will serve 12.

Hot Chocolate

¼ cup cocoa	1 quart milk
½ cup sugar	1 t vanilla
¼ cup boiling water	

Blend cocoa and sugar in a sauce pan. Add the boiling water and stir. Heat this mixture on medium high, stirring constantly until a syrup forms and bubbles. When all is nicely mixed, add the milk, scald, remove from stove, and add vanilla. Fill up a mug and pray for snow!

Party Foods

The next variation which their visit afforded was produced by the entrance of servants with cold meat, cake, and a variety of fruits in season. There was now employment for the whole party; for though they could not all talk, they could all eat; and the beautiful pyramids of grapes, nectarines, and peaches soon collected them round the table.

~from Pride and Prejudice, by Jane Austen

No hostess knows for certain that all her guests are compatible. Finger foods and tempting drinks help to blend a disparate party and to ease guests over any little social hurdles. As they were in Jane Austen's day, cold meat, cake, and fruit are good basic items at a tea table. For example, a chilled turkey breast, a cold, thinly-sliced baked ham, and a hot roast beef are delicious when accompanied by homemade breads and biscuits. Cakes of every variety and shape are pleasant to taste and pretty to look at; strawberries dipped in chocolate and grapes sprinkled with powdered sugar are colorful and appetizing. If you want something different, cold, boiled shrimp on a bed of ice, shrimp molds, and tasteful crab dishes always disappear rapidly from the tea table.

Crab Meat Balls

2 cups fresh crab meat
½ t lemon juice
1 T mayonnaise
½ pint cream
1 T chopped pimento
1 T chopped parsley
½ t salt
1 cup cracker meal

Mix all ingredients except cracker meal and cream. Shape into balls. Roll in cream and then in cracker meal and fry in deep fat until brown. (Fry at 365° for about 2 minutes.)

Crab Dip

1 cup Hellman's Mayonnaise
½ cup sour cream
1 T chopped parsley
1-6 ½ oz can crab, drained, or one cup fresh, chilled crab
1 T sherry
1 t lemon juice
Salt and pepper to taste

Combine all ingredients and chill two hours before serving with crackers or crisp raw vegetables.

Shrimp Dip

1- 8 oz package cream cheese
1 pound shrimp, boiled, chilled & chopped
Juice of one lemon

1 small Vidalia onion, grated
1 cup mayonnaise

Mix and serve as dip with Triscuits or other crisp crackers.

Shrimp Mold

1 can tomato soup, heated
1 -8 oz package cream cheese
1½ packages unflavored gelatin
1/3 cup cold water

1 med. onion finely chopped
1 cup cooked shrimp
   (chilled and finely chopped)
1 cup mayonnaise

Heat soup and cream cheese in top of double boiler. Dissolve gelatin in cold water and add to hot mixture. Cool. Add all other ingredients and chill. Mold in a shrimp mold and decorate with olives, etc.

Shrimp in Bacon

Wrap shelled and deveined raw shrimp in half slices of bacon. Fasten ends with toothpick. Grill in broiler or bake in hot oven until shrimp is pink and bacon is crisp. Replace charred toothpicks with fresh cocktail picks.

Spinach Dip I

1 cup sour cream   1 cup mayonnaise
1 package Knox dry vegetable soup mix   1 small grated onion
1 can water chestnuts, drained and chopped
1 package frozen chopped spinach, cooked, cooled, and squeezed dry.

Mix all, chill, and serve with buttery crackers.

Both Helen and I were required to "clean up our plates" and to taste everything new. My mother served a number of tempting spinach dishes, including this spinach dip. She also loved to tell the story of a lazy friend, who usually served her husband canned spinach. The woman declared, "I think I like canned spinach better than fresh."

"So do I," her husband said. "It doesn't have as much grit in it."

Spinach Dip II

1 package frozen chopped spinach, thawed, drained, and squeezed dry
1 cup mayonnaise   1 cup sour cream
1-3 oz package cream cheese   2 t Worcestershire sauce
1 t seasoned salt   1 small onion, minced

Mix all together, chill, and serve with a variety of crackers.

Stuffed Mushrooms

1/2 pound mushrooms, washed, with stems removed

1 small onion, chopped fine   3 T cottage cheese

1/4 cup soft bread crumbs   Butter

Sautè the mushroom stems and onions in butter. Add bread crumbs. Remove from heat and add cheese. Stuff mushroom caps with mixture and broil lightly. Serve hot.

Pecan and Cream Cheese Stuffed Dates

½ cup softened cream cheese mixed with ½ cup finely chopped pecans

24 dates   8 slices bacon

Stuff the dates with cream cheese mixture.
Place dates on a baking sheet lined with foil.
Preheat the oven to 350°.
Bake the dates 5 minutes. Remove to plate.
Cut bacon into thirds crosswise, and bake until done, but not crisp.
Wrap each stuffed date with bacon, and secure it with a toothpick.
Place your stuffed dates on a foil-lined baking sheet.
Bake the wrapped dates about six minutes.
Turn dates, and bake 5 minutes more.

Raw Vegetable Dip

2/3 pint Hellmann's Mayonnaise   2 T honey

7 drops Tabasco   2 T catsup

1 T lemon juice   1 t curry powder

2 T minced onion

Mix all ingredients, chill at least one hour, and serve with raw vegetables.

Cheese Delights

4 oz extra sharp cheddar cheese, grated
¼ cup butter, softened
½ cup flour
¼ t white pepper
Paprika to taste

Cream together cheese and butter. Blend in flour and pepper. Form into balls the size of marbles. Place on ungreased cookie sheet and flatten with a fork to make a waffle design. Sprinkle with paprika. Chill in refrigerator several hours. Bake at 450° for 8-10 minutes until brown. Serve hot. This recipe makes three dozen.

These little cheese wafers are good with cold drinks or with raw vegetables.

Toasted Cheese Canapés

20 slices white bread
2 T butter
2 egg whites, beaten stiff
1 ¼ cups coarsely grated Swiss cheese
2/3 cup sliced stuffed olives, chopped
1 t minced parsley
½ t salt
¼ t pepper
3 slices diced cooked bacon

Cut twenty bread rounds. Toast on one side. Brush untoasted side with butter. Into egg whites fold cheese, olives, parsley (minced), salt, and pepper. Spoon this mixture on to buttered side of bread rounds. Sprinkle finely diced bacon on top of each. Place on broiler pan 4 or 5 inches from heat for 5 minutes or until bacon browns and cheese melts.

Sardine Puffs

Yes, that's it! Sardines. We couldn't resist adding my mother's depression-era appetizer, featuring the lowly and poor sardine as the main ingredient. (Could sardines be worse than caviar?)

8 slices bread	4 t prepared mustard
4 cans (3 1/2 oz) sardines	2 t lemon juice
2/3 cup mayonnaise	1 t curry powder
2 T minced onion	2 egg whites

Cut bread diagonally into four pieces. Toast bread on one side. Arrange well drained sardines on untoasted side. Blend mayonnaise, onion, mustard, lemon juice, and curry powder. Fold in stiffly beaten egg whites. Spread mixture over the sardines, covering sardines and bread. Bake in a hot oven 400° for five or ten minutes, until puffy and golden brown. Serve immediately. Makes 32 puffs.

If you dare to serve this dish, don't reveal the main ingredient!

Toasted Pecans

Beat 1 egg white until frothy. Add 1 cup brown sugar. Dip pecan halves into mixture. Bake at 225° until crisp, about 20 minutes.

The concoction that follows, Cocktail Meat Balls, was a staple at my mother's bridge and church parties. To hear her describe the preparation of this delicacy was almost as much fun as eating the steaming meatballs. They were so delicious that I never found a single one in a pot plant. My mother took pride in the secret ingredient: grape jelly!

Cocktail Meat Balls

Meat Mixture:

2 pounds ground chuck	1/4 t pepper
1 large onion, chopped fine	1/4 t salt
1/4 t garlic salt	1/8 cup catsup
1 egg	

Mix onion, seasoning, egg, and catsup. Add chuck and mix well. Make into balls the size of marbles and place in electric frying pan.

Sauce:

1/2 cup Welch's grape jelly	1/2 cup red wine
2 bottles Heinz chili sauce	

Mix ingredients for sauce well and pour over meatballs. Simmer on lowest heat (200°-250°) for three hours. When done, keep hot in a crock pot until you serve.

Peanut Butter Strips

    1 cup each Wesson oil and peanut butter (You may need more.)
    1 T honey
    1 loaf of bread cut into strips

Cut the crusts off each slice of bread and set aside. Cut remaining bread into strips about the size of your little finger. (This task will be easier if you use an electric knife.) Dry out strips and crusts in a very slow oven (250°) but do not brown. When the <u>crusts</u> are dry, roll them into a fine meal with a rolling pin, or crush them in a food processor.

Dip the dried <u>strips</u> into a mixture made from equal parts of oil and peanut butter plus 1 tablespoon honey (optional). After rolling the strips in the meal, set aside, dry, and store in airtight container.

Peanut butter strips were served at every one of my mother's parties, and she was a frequent hostess. These strips are not hard to make, but preparation takes time.

Smoked Salmon Cheese Cake

½ cup dried, unflavored bread crumbs	¼ cup chopped chives
1 cup and 1/3 cup Parmesan cheese	2 t lemon zest
½ stick unsalted butter, soft	½ t salt
2 pounds cream cheese, soft	Freshly ground black pepper
4 large eggs	1 cup sour cream
¼ cup chopped parsley	12 oz smoked salmon chopped

                                                              (OVER NEXT PAGE)

Preheat the oven to 350°. Prepare a 9 X 3 cake pan (not a cheesecake pan) with cooking spray and parchment paper. Blend together the bread crumbs, 1 cup Parmesan cheese, and butter in a small bowl. Press the mixture evenly into the bottom of the cake pan. Set aside. Place the cream cheese in large bowl of electric mixer. With the flat paddle, beat the cream cheese on medium speed until light and fluffy. Beat in the remaining Parmesan cheese. Add the eggs, one at a time, beating after each. Beat in chives and parsley, lemon zest, salt, and pepper. Mix well. Stir in the sour cream by hand and fold in the chopped salmon.

Pour the batter into the pan and smooth the top with a small offset spatula. Place the cake pan in a larger pan filled with 1 inch hot water. Bake about 30 to 40 minutes. The cake should be set around the edges, but still creamy and soft in the middle. Turn the oven off and let cake cool in the oven. Remove the cake from the oven, cool completely on a rack, then refrigerate it overnight or longer. This recipe may be prepared two days ahead. Wrap it tightly and store in refrigerator, still in its pan. Turn cake out on a flat surface. Remove parchment, and, using another flat plate, flip cake gently over again. Serve chilled with toast points. This recipe was one of Don's favorites and one of the special dishes he requested for his birthday.

Dill Toast Points

35 thin slices white bread	1/3 cup olive oil
½ stick unsalted butter	2 T dried dill

Preheat oven to 350°. Line a baking sheet with parchment paper. Remove crusts from the bread and cut each slice in half, diagonally. (Use electric knife.) Melt butter in small saucepan and stir in the olive oil and dill. Brush both sides of the bread triangles with this mixture. Place on baking sheet and bake 10 minutes. Store at room temperature until needed. Be careful not to break them.

Corn Dog Muffins

1 box Martha White or Jiffy corn muffin mix
1 cup shredded cheddar cheese
3 or 4 hot dogs, quartered and chopped
½ cup milk
1 egg

Mix all together. Spray muffin pans with cooking spray. Divide batter into 12 cup muffin pan. Bake at 400° for 20 minutes. Serve with catsup and mustard.

Sausage Phyllo Cups

1 pound sausage meat
3 or 4 green onions, finely chopped
2-8 oz cream cheese
5 packages phyllo shells

Brown sausage and drain. Add softened cream cheese and onion. Mix well. Put a small scoop of mixture in each phyllo shell. Bake at 350° for 10-15 minutes. Makes 60 individual cups.

Tortilla Roll-Ups

1 package super-size flour tortillas
2-8oz packages cream cheese, softened
¼ cup chopped black olives
½ cup mild salsa
2 T chopped green onions

Put cream cheese, salsa, and onions in food processor. Mix well. Pour into bowl and mix in olives. Spread mixture in a thin layer on each tortilla and roll up tightly. Wrap each roll in wax paper and refrigerate several hours or overnight. Slice into ¾ inch pieces and serve with salsa.

Pecan Pie Muffins

1 1/3 stick butter, melted
1 cup packed brown sugar
1 cup chopped pecans
½ cup all-purpose flour
2 eggs, beaten

Melt butter and cool. Beat eggs and add to butter. Mix together. Mix together flour, brown sugar, and nuts. Add butter and egg mixture. Mix well. Spray muffin tins, put liners in and spray also (muffins will stick if liners are not sprayed). Fill with mixture. Bake at 350° for 20-25 minutes. Cool on wire rack. Makes 1 dozen.

Helen's Divinity

2 ½ cups sugar
½ cup white Karo syrup
¼ cup water
3 egg whites, beaten until fluffy

1 t vanilla
1/8 t salt
1 cup chopped pecans

Combine sugar, Karo syrup, and water. Bring to boil. Cover and let boil 3 minutes. Uncover and cook to 250°. Pour over beaten egg whites and salt. Add vanilla. Beat until mixture holds shape. (May take up to an hour depending on the weather...low humidity is best!) Add pecans and drop by teaspoon onto wax paper. Let dry until candy is not sticky.

Fudge

4 cups sugar
1 1/3 cup canned milk
1 cup butter
12 oz semi-sweet chocolate chips

7 oz marshmallow cream
2 cups chopped pecans
1 t vanilla

Line a 13x9x2 pan with foil, then spray.

Butter the sides of heavy 3 quart pot. Mix sugar, milk, and butter and cook over medium heat to boiling. Cook to 236° on candy thermometer, stirring constantly. Remove from heat. Add chocolate chips, marshmallow cream, and vanilla. Stir until chocolate melts. Add pecans. Spread into pan. Score while warm. After it cools, cut into pieces.

Party Beverages

"Life starts all over when things get cool again in the fall."
    Jordan Baker, in *The Great Gatsby*, by F. Scott Fitzgerald

Jordan Baker was right. A crisp autumn day heralds life-changing events, both grand and small. The season brings forth hot drinks like dark, rich coffees, comforting or exotic teas, and hot chocolate. A traditional favorite for ringing in winter is Russian Tea. In the 1950's, Russian Tea was quite fashionable, but the pleasure it once gave was destroyed when "Tang" came on the market. A bad recipe imitating Russian Tea was devised and handed about, using Tang, cinnamon, and ground cloves. Tang was a dreadful drink, but many people used it as a substitute ingredient for citrus flavors. Genuine Russian Tea, unlike its imitation, is delicious, deeply satisfying, and welcome at anytime, but especially on a cold day.

Russian Tea

3 lemons	15 whole cloves
4 oranges	2 tea bags (family size)
2 cups pineapple juice	2 cups sugar
2 quarts water (8 cups)	

Squeeze lemons and oranges, add pineapple juice, and set aside. Boil water and add the cloves in a bag or in a small stainless steel strainer with a screw-on top. Add tea bags and steep 15 minutes. Remove tea bags and cloves and add sugar, stirring well. Add the fruit juices and serve hot.

Once I attended an impressive social function at the country club in Spartanburg, South Carolina. I saw the social leader of the community, Fannie Louise Holcombe, approach the swinging kitchen door with fire in her eyes. Encountering a server, Mrs. Holcombe ordered that the punch be removed from its perch at the head of the table.

"Take this punch back to the kitchen," she said, in a voice that brooked no argument. "It's too sweet, and it's not cold enough."

If you go to a party, and you are not into the champagne, you will want a cup of cold, cold punch. It is shocking how many times you can't find one!

Ann's Favorite Punch

1 small can frozen lemonade
1 can frozen orange juice (12 oz), dissolved in 1 small can water
1-46 oz can pineapple juice, unsweetened
1-32 ounce bottle of ginger ale

Pour all together over lots of crushed ice. If you wish, you may make the ice from apple juice. Pour ginger ale into the punch bowl. Keep cool!

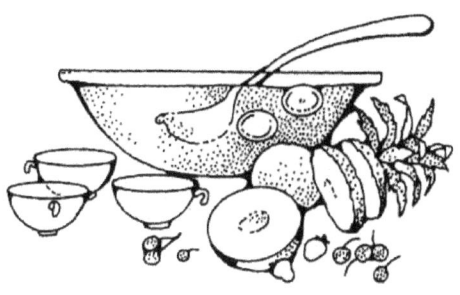

Helen's Favorite Punch

2 tubs of Raspberry Ice Crystal Light (look in Kool Aid section)
¾ cup of sugar
1-46 oz can of pineapple juice
¼ t almond flavoring
1 quart ginger ale, chilled, added when ready to serve

Mix these ingredients together and pour into gallon jug. Finish filling jug with water and chill. When ready to serve, pour into a punch bowl and add ginger ale. Serve very cold over ice. You may make flavored ice by freezing a bit of the Crystal Light mixture.

When her family was at home, Helen always had this punch ready in the refrigerator.

Mocha Punch

Mocha punch requires a large punch bowl and is appropriate for any meal and in any weather! It is especially delightful when one is serving outside or on the porch or veranda.

1-4 oz jar instant coffee granules	2 cups boiling water
1 gallon milk	1 pint whipping cream
½ gallon vanilla ice cream	½ gallon chocolate ice cream

Pour the boiling water into the coffee granules. Allow to cool, then chill in refrigerator. When ready to prepare the first punch bowl, pour about half this coffee mixture into the punch bowl. Add half the cold milk and stir. Scoop in ice cream as needed, being sure that some of each flavor of ice cream is in the bowl. Top with the whipped cream, sprinkle with nutmeg. Serve in punch cups or wine glasses.

Sox Hemperley's Famous Egg Nog

12 eggs, separated	12 T sugar
12 T Seagram 7 Whiskey	1 pint heavy whipping cream

Separate eggs, putting yolks in one bowl and whites in another. Beat the yolks at high speed of mixer (hand mixer or standing mixer) until thick. Then add the whiskey slowly, and continue beating until almost stiff. Clean and dry beaters.

Beat the egg whites until they begin to thicken. Then gradually add sugar, one tablespoon at a time, until all sugar is gone. Beat until peaks form, and meringue will not move when you turn bowl on its side. Whip cream until stiff. Fold the meringue into the yolk mixture and fold whipped cream into mixture. Serve in punch cups and eat with a spoon.

Sandwiches

In people's eyes, in the swing, tramp, and trudge; in the bellow and uproar; the carriages, motor cars, omnibuses, vans, sandwich men shuffling and swinging; brass bands, barrel organs; in the triumph and the jingle and the strange high singing of some aeroplane overheard was what she loved: life; London; this moment in June.

—from *Mrs. Dalloway,* by Virginia Wolfe

Sandwiches are great English and American fare, and everyone working late or studying hard warms to the idea of "sending out for sandwiches and coffee." On the streets of London or New York, or indeed in many parks and fairs, strollers delight in stopping for hot dogs or sausage buns from a street vendor, a tradition familiar since before the time of Dickens.

In my mother's family there were two kinds of sandwiches: those we packed and took to school, on a train, or to a picnic; and those dainty morsels we prepared for guests. These party-sandwiches are the ones that evoke feelings of anticipation or desperation. The brilliantly colored picture of a tea table in a recipe book inspires, while the first spooning of a sandwich filling on a round of bread intimidates—especially when you know there are four hundred to go. Miss Helen has infinite patience with these dainty morsels, and she has a knack for making sandwiches as pretty as they are good to eat.

I first began to take an interest in fancy sandwiches when I was about thirteen years old. Cousin Margaret Burch lived with my family in Atlanta, and she was my idea of everything sophisticated and lovely. She had beautiful hair, a slim figure, spoke Spanish, and worked at Eastern Airlines during the hectic traveling days of World War II. She went out with dashing service men every weekend.

Cousin Margaret was in a sorority, and she invited me to attend a meeting with her. At this meeting, a chef was demonstrating how to make a sandwich loaf for a party. Somehow, I never forgot this recipe, and for many years, I have always had a "Party Sandwich Loaf" when I gave a tea.

I have certainly made more lunch box sandwiches than party sandwiches over the years; but whether you are making fancy sandwiches for a party or substantial ones for a lunch box, be sure to spread the bread with soft butter. When the sandwiches are prepared, refrigerate. The butter becomes firm and serves as a binder, preventing the spread from soaking into the bread itself. Chilled in this manner, a sandwich will remain quite cool in the lunch box or on the serving table for three or four hours.

Party Sandwich Loaf

<u>One loaf of bread</u>, sliced lengthwise, end to end, so that you have rectangular slices that can be stacked like a cake.

<u>Three sandwich fillings</u>: egg salad, chicken salad, and ham salad

<u>Two eight ounce packages cream cheese</u>, softened and whipped

Egg Salad: Place six eggs in cold water. Bring to a boil. Cover, remove from heat, and allow to sit 20 minutes. Pour cold water over eggs to cool. Peel and mash with a table fork. Add about 1/3 cup of mayonnaise. Add 1 T sweet pickle relish, drained, and 2 ribs celery, chopped. Salt and pepper to taste. Blend.

Ham Salad: From a baked ham, cut several slices. Chop in food processor until fairly fine. When you have about 1 ½ cups add 1 T Durkees, 1/3 cup mayonnaise, 2 T dill relish, drained, and 1 t. mustard.

Chicken Salad: Cook a whole chicken gently in a small amount of water. Use a large cooking pot with a well-fitting lid; the cooking will require at least an hour. Pick chicken from bone, discarding objectionable parts. Put in food processor, but stop when the chicken is nicely chopped. Add ½ cup mayonnaise, ½ of a small Vidalia onion, grated, 3 ribs celery, and ½ cup chopped bread and butter pickles. (You may be able to have the chicken cooked at the deli, if you prefer.)

Cut the crust from the bread, which has been sliced lengthwise. Butter every exposed side. Spread the fillings on the bread slices, stacking the loaves and alternating the fillings. Wrap in plastic wrap and store in refrigerator overnight. Before serving, frost with cream cheese. Place on a beautiful plate and decorate with pimento, mint, and other herbs. Slice as you would a cake. Beautiful!

Ham and Cheese Rolls

Buy two packages of rolls, in foil pans, from the bread aisle. (These rolls have 24 pieces, "fat finger" size.)

½ pound of sandwich ham
1 small onion, grated   1/3 cup poppy seed
2 T mustard   ½ pound cheddar cheese, grated
2 sticks butter   ½ pound mozzarella cheese, grated

Remove rolls from pan and slice them end to end, but do not separate the rolls from each other. Melt butter; add poppy seed, mustard, and onion. Return bottom half of cut rolls to pan. Brush cut sides of tops and bottoms of rolls with the butter mixture. Layer ham on top of rolls in pan. Sprinkle with both kinds of cheese. Add roll top to rolls in pan. Now, cut between each roll! Cover with foil, and refrigerate overnight. When ready, bake 30 minutes at 350°, while still covered. These are delicious served hot.

Cream Cheese and Onion Spread

Cream cheese and onion sandwiches are delicious for afternoon tea.

1 -8 oz package cream cheese, whipped with 2 T mayonnaise
2 T finely chopped Vidalia onion
½ cup pecans, finely chopped

Mix ingredients together. Cut bread into desired shapes. Cover with above mixture.

Scones

For a ladies' party occasion, especially an afternoon tea, nothing is finer than a plate of scones.

4 cups White Lily self-rising flour	1 large egg
¼ cup sugar	Milk, optional
½ t cream of tartar	1 t cinnamon sugar, optional
2/3 cup butter	1 1/3 cups half and half

Preheat oven to 425°. Sift together flour, sugar, and cream of tartar. Cut butter into flour mixture with a pastry blender, moving bowl as you cut, just as you would for a biscuit. In second bowl, beat together cream and egg; add these liquids to flour/sugar/butter mixture. Mix the dough lightly with a blending fork, then turn out on a floured surface. Knead ten times, and roll out to about ½ inch thickness. Cut rounds with a biscuit cutter. (Do not twist the cutter as you cut.)

If you want plain scones to serve with cream and jam, do not add cinnamon sugar. If you want the cinnamon scones, brush the tops of the scones with milk and sprinkle with cinnamon sugar. Serve the cinnamon scones with apple butter.

Scones are nice served with mock Devonshire cream instead of butter. Whip 1 pint of heavy whipping cream until stiff; blend in 1 tablespoon of sugar and ½ cup of sour cream. Serve with jam on the bread plate, and pass the scones.

Cheese Tomato Sandwich

These sandwiches are good for "tea time with the kids."

Toast bread slices on one side in broiler. Top each untoasted side with a slice of tomato. Cover the slices with generous amounts of crumbled cheddar or Swiss cheese. Sprinkle several drops of Worcestershire sauce on cheese. Broil until cheese begins to melt. Serve hot.

Date Nut Sandwich Filling

½ cup finely chopped dates
¼ cup chopped nuts
6 T orange juice
1-3 oz package cream cheese, softened.

Mix well and use for sandwich spread on banana bread or raisin bread. This recipe is easy to double or triple.

Pimento Cheese

1-8 oz package cheddar cheese
1-8 oz package cream cheese
1 medium jar diced pimentos
¼ to ½ cup mayonnaise

Grate the cheddar cheese (by hand or in food processor) and put aside. In food processor, place cream cheese which is at room temperature. Blend with mayonnaise. Add cheddar until all is nicely blended. Add pimentos, and blend only briefly, so that some red will still appear. For the tea table, trim the crusts from a loaf of bread. Flatten each slice of bread by rolling from side to side with a rolling pen. Spread the pimento cheese mixture on one side of each slice. Roll up each slice as you would a jelly roll. Wrap in plastic wrap and foil and refrigerate. Before party time, remove from refrigerator, slice each roll diagonally, and place on a serving plate. Decorate with parsley.

Pimento cheese is the most popular sandwich spread in the South. A sandwich of pimento cheese is delicious toasted under the broiler. A picnic featuring fried chicken is almost never served without including pimento cheese sandwiches.

Cucumber Sandwiches

"Sir, there are no cucumbers in the market this morning, even for ready money!"

~from The Importance of Being Ernest, by Oscar Wilde

Never have a tea without cucumber sandwiches!

Cut sandwich rounds from white bread slices with small biscuit cutter. Spread these with cream cheese, which has been softened and mixed with a trace of mayonnaise. Peel cucumbers. Place a cucumber on each round. Put on a tea tray and adorn with mint or dill.

Pineapple Sandwiches

Children love these pineapple sandwiches for a "proper tea." Chill a can of sliced pineapple. Drain pineapple rings on paper towels. With a large biscuit cutter, cut bread slices into rounds. Mix ¼ cup softened cream cheese with 1 cup of Hellman's mayonnaise and spread on bread rounds. Top with a slice of pineapple. Place a maraschino cherry in the center.

Breads and Pastries

Which of you shall have a friend, and shall go unto him at midnight, and say unto him, Friend, lend me three loaves; For a friend of mine in his journey is come to me, and I have nothing to set before him? And he from within shall answer and say, Trouble me not: the door is now shut, and my children are with me in bed; I cannot rise up and give thee. I say unto you, Though he will not rise and give him, because he is his friend, yet because of his importunity he will rise and give him as many as he needeth.

~Luke 11:5-8, *The King James Bible*

Once my parents and my brother and I arrived at Helen's childhood home late at night, on Christmas Eve. We opened the unlocked door and were overwhelmed with the fragrance of the Christmas pine. This little-used front room, where the tree always stood, was cold and dark, but light from the kerosene lamps and the fireplace flickered under and around the next door. I stood still for a moment in my excitement. We knew that warmth and wonderful food awaited us in the inner room, and that hot bread would be brought to the table for the late supper. And we knew that they would be biscuits, the bread of the South. Years later, in my own home, I often waited for returning family. I always had a pot of simmering soup and hot biscuits ready, and I kept the butter soft. A Southern lady knows what is expected of her. As far as I remember, I never had to arouse the neighbors to ask for bread, though it would have been a blessing to them had I done so.

Angel Biscuits

5 cups self rising flour (White Lily)   1 cup Crisco

1/3 cup sugar   2 cups buttermilk

1 t baking soda

2 packages yeast, dissolved into ¼ cup lukewarm water

Combine dry ingredients. Cut in shortening. Stir yeast/water into lukewarm buttermilk. Add combined liquids to dry ingredients and blend. Roll out and cut as desired, or make into Parker House Rolls. (Cut dough with a large biscuit cutter, and fold over in center.) Place rolls on baking sheet and set in warm place to rise. (Rising takes about one hour.) Bake at 450° until nicely browned.

Sour Cream Gems

2 cups self rising flour (unsifted)   1 cup sour cream

1 cup butter (not margarine) at room temperature

Measure the two cups unsifted flour into sifter, sift into bowl. Cut in butter with pastry blender, fork, or two knives. Add sour cream. Stir until the flour/butter mixture is moistened. Spoon into greased miniature muffin pans. Bake at 350° about 20 minutes, until golden brown. These biscuits are great, and so easy!

Quick Rolls

1 package yeast	1/2 cup boiling water
1/2 cup warm water	1 egg
1/4 cup sugar	1 t salt
1/2 cup shortening	3 1/2 cups sifted flour

Empty yeast in warm water, stir well and set aside. Cream sugar and shortening well. Pour boiling water on mixture of sugar and shortening. Mix well and allow to cool slightly. Add beaten egg and, gradually, half of the flour and mix well. Add warm water and yeast, remaining flour and salt. Roll out on floured board and cut in round shapes. Place on ungreased baking sheet. Let rise one hour. Bake at 400° until nicely browned.

Perfectly Easy Dinner Rolls

1 cup warm water (105 to 115 F)	3 eggs
2 packages active dry yeast (not rapid rise)	1 t salt
½ cup butter, melted	4 ½ cups all-purpose flour
½ cup sugar	Additional melted butter

Combine warm water and yeast in a large bowl. Let the mixture stand until yeast is foamy, about 5 minutes. Stir in melted butter, sugar, eggs, and salt. Beat in flour, one cup at a time, until dough is too stiff to mix. (Some of the flour may not be needed.) Cover and refrigerate for two hours, or up to four days. Grease a 13 X 9 inch baking pan, turn the chilled dough out on to a lightly floured board or pastry cloth. Divide dough into 24 equal pieces. Roll each piece into a smooth, round ball. Place balls in even rows in prepared pan. Cover and let rise until doubled in volume, about one hour. Bake in preheated 400° degree oven 15-20 minutes, or until golden brown. Serve with soft butter.

Ice Box Rolls

1 package yeast, ½ cup warm water	2 t salt
1 cup scalded milk	1 cup cooked potatoes, mashed
2/3 cup Crisco	2 eggs, well beaten
½ cup sugar	Flour to make stiff dough

Dissolve yeast in lukewarm water; set aside. To the <u>scalded</u> milk, add the Crisco, sugar, salt, and mashed up potatoes. When cool, add yeast mixture. Mix well and add eggs. Stir about three cups sifted flour into potato/egg mixture. Sift in more flour, ¼ to ½ cup at the time, until the mixture is the consistency of a soft biscuit dough. (Be careful adding flour, as mixture should not be too stiff.) Place in bowl large enough to allow for rising. Rub over with butter. Place in refrigerator. When ready to use, make into rolls and let rise until double. (About two hours.) Bake at 425° until nicely browned.

Once on Christmas day, Mother made these rolls instead of her usual biscuits. Only our cousin, Buster Travis, was disappointed. "If I'd been a bettin' man," he said, "I would have bet there'd be biscuits on this table today!" From that holiday on, we had both rolls and biscuits.

Rolls

1 cup Crisco	2 eggs, beaten
1 cup boiling water	2 packages dry yeast
½ cup sugar	1 cup lukewarm water
1½ t salt	6 cups flour, sifted

Mix Crisco, boiling water, sugar, and salt until Crisco is melted. Let stand until lukewarm. Add eggs and yeast and lukewarm water. Add flour. Beat thoroughly. Put in refrigerator overnight. Roll out and cut. Let rise two hours before baking at 400° until nice and brown.

Riz Biscuits

2 ½ cups self rising flour, sifted
1/4 t baking soda
3 T sugar

1 package yeast
1 cup lukewarm buttermilk
1/3 cup Crisco

Sift together flour, soda, and sugar. Dissolve yeast in buttermilk. Cut shortening into flour. Stir buttermilk into flour mixture. Quickly turn on cloth and knead until smooth. Roll to 1/4 inch thickness, cut with biscuit cutter, and place on a greased baking sheet. Brush top of each round with butter. Place a second biscuit on top, and brush with butter. Place in a warm place, covered with greased wax paper, for one hour. Biscuits will double. Bake at 375° for 12-15 minutes.

Southern Cream Biscuits

2 ½ cups all purpose flour
2 T baking powder
1 t salt

1 stick unsalted butter, cut up
1-1 ¼ cups whipping cream

Sift flour with baking powder and salt. Cut in butter until mixture looks like coarse meal. Add 1 cup whipping cream, and more if necessary. Roll out to ½ inch thickness and cut with biscuit cutter. Put on ungreased baking sheet ½ inches apart. Bake at 400° until golden brown, about 15-20 minutes. Serve immediately.

Cheddar Garlic Drop Biscuits

2 cups White Lily self-rising flour
¼ cup Crisco
1 cup shredded cheddar cheese
¾ cup milk or buttermilk
¼ cup butter, softened
½ t garlic powder

Preheat oven to 450°. Line baking sheet with parchment or foil, and spray lightly with non-stick cooking spray. Measure flour into large bowl. Add shortening, and cut into flour with a pastry cutter. Stir in cheese and milk, stirring only enough to moisten flour and hold dough together. Drop by rounded soup spoon onto the prepared baking sheet. Bake 8 to 10 minutes, or until tops are golden brown. Combine butter and garlic powder, and brush on top of hot biscuits.

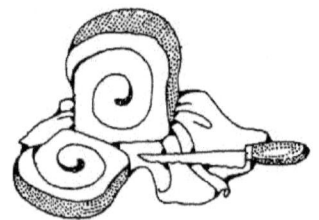

Giant Popovers

6 T butter
2 cups milk
1 t salt
6 eggs
2 cups all-purpose flour
Vegetable oil spray

About 1 ½ hours before serving, melt butter. Heat oven to 375°. In large bowl with mixer at low speed, beat eggs until frothy. Beat in milk, butter, flour and salt. Spray 6 to 8 (1-cup) ramekins with vegetable oil. Fill each ¾ full with batter. Bake 1 hour. Pull from oven and quickly make a slit in the top of each popover to let out the steam. Return to the oven for 10 minutes. Serve piping hot.

Sweet Potato Bread

1 quart cooked, mashed sweet potatoes
3 T flour
1 stick butter, melted

4 eggs
2 ½ cups sugar
1 t vanilla

Mix all ingredients and pour into a greased 9x15 pan. Bake at 350° about 1 hour until firm

Cranberry Nut Bread

2 cups sifted all purpose flour
1 t baking soda
1 t salt
3/4 cup sugar
1 egg
1/3 cup orange juice

3 T white vinegar plus
    water to make 2/3 cup
1 t grated orange rind
1/4 cup Wesson oil
1 cup chopped cranberries
1 cup chopped nuts

Sift flour, baking soda, salt, and sugar. Set aside. Beat egg and add liquids, grated orange rind, and melted shortening. Add all at once to flour mixture and stir until flour is just dampened. Add cranberries and nuts. Bake in greased loaf pan at 350° for about 1 hour. Cool 10 minutes before turning out.

Cranberry Nut Bread was Mother's holiday gift bread. It is pretty when cut, looks festive, and tastes delicious!

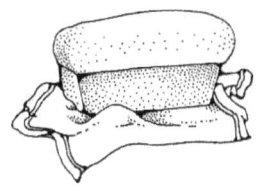

Date Nut Bread

1 egg
1/4 cup sugar
1/2 cup dates, chopped
1/2 cup nuts, chopped

2 cups all purpose flour
4 t baking powder
1/2 t salt
1 cup milk

Beat eggs and add sugar. Add dates and nuts. Sift dry ingredients together and add alternately with milk. Bake in loaf pan at 350° for 45 minutes.

Cherry Nut Bread

2 ¼ cups flour
3 t baking powder
1 t salt
½ t nutmeg
½ cup sugar
½ cup butter

½ cup chopped candied cherries
½ cup chopped pecans
¾ cup milk
3 eggs, separated
¼ cup sugar

Sift flour with baking powder, salt, nutmeg, and ½ cup sugar. Cut in butter with pastry blender and stir in cherries and nuts. Beat milk with egg yolks and stir into flour mixture. Beat egg whites until soft peaks form. Gradually add ¼ cup sugar and continue beating until stiff. Fold into batter. Bake in a greased loaf pan for 1 hour at 350°.

Banana Nut Bread

1 cup Crisco
2 cups sugar
4 eggs
6 small bananas, or 4 large

4 scant cups self-rising flour
1 cup chopped pecans
½ cup chopped raisins, optional

Cream shortening and sugar until light. Add eggs, beating after each, and then the mashed banana. Add flour, ½ cup at the time, beating gently. Add nuts and fruit and blend. Grease and flour 2 large loaf pans or 1 tube pan. Pour batter into pan. Bake at 350° for 1 hour or until done. Cool 10 minutes and turn out.

Strawberry Nut Bread

1 cup soft butter
1 ½ cups sugar
1/4 t lemon juice
4 eggs
3 cups sifted flour
1 t salt

1 t cream tartar
½ t baking soda
1 cup strawberry jam
½ cup sour cream
1 cup chopped nuts
1 t vanilla

Cream butter, sugar, and lemon. Beat until light and fluffy. Add eggs, one at a time, beating well after each addition. In separate bowl, combine flour, salt, soda, and cream of tartar. Combine strawberry jam and sour cream, and add to creamed mixture alternately with dry mixture. Add nuts and vanilla. Pour into four greased and floured 7 X 3X 2 inch loaf pans. Bake in 350° oven for 55-60 minutes. Remove from pan immediately.

Pumpkin Bread

2 cans pumpkin	½ t baking powder
3 cups sugar	2 t salt
4 eggs	2 t baking soda
1 cup oil	3 ½ cups plain flour
1 cup water	¼ t cloves
½ t cinnamon	2 cups nuts, chopped
¼ t nutmeg	

Beat sugar gradually into pumpkin. Beat eggs until thick and lemon colored. Add to pumpkin mix. Add oil and water. Mix dry ingredients together and combine with wet mixture. Fold in nuts. Pour into three greased loaf pans. Bake at 325° for 1 hour and 10 minutes.

Pie Pastry I

3 cups plain flour, sifted with ½ t salt
1 cup Crisco
½ cup ice water
(This recipe makes two crusts.)

Blend Crisco into flour with pastry blender. Add water slowly until mix makes a stiff dough. Roll out in a circle an inch larger than pie plate. Move to pie plate, prick with a fork, and bake at 425° for 12-15 minutes. Do not prick when using crust for custard and fruit fillings. Instead, fill uncooked crust, and bake.

Pie Pastry II

3 cups all purpose flour

½ t salt

1 t baking powder

1 cup Crisco, frozen

1/3 cup milk

1 egg, beaten

Sift flour with salt and baking powder. Cut in shortening. Add milk to beaten egg, then add to flour mix. If mixture seems dry, add another T milk. If too moist, work in a little flour. Divide dough in half. (This recipe makes two crusts.) Fit into pie plate, prick with fork, bake at 475° for 8-10 minutes.

When making a pie crust, use enough flour on the board to roll the dough out easily. Roll from the center toward the edge. When you have a nice circle, flip dough on to rolling pin and then place it in the pie plate.

Aunt Christine's Apple Walnut Muffins

¾ cup oil

1 cup sugar

2 eggs

2 cups all purpose flour

¾ t baking soda

½ t salt

¾ t cinnamon

1 t vanilla

½ cup chopped walnuts

1 ½ cups chopped apples

Beat oil and sugar together for 2 minutes in electric mixer. Add eggs and beat. Sift together flour, soda, salt, and cinnamon and add to liquids. Stir in walnuts and apples last. Pour into prepared muffin pans, or line pans with cupcake papers. Fill muffin cups ½ full. Bake at 400° for about 18 minutes. When muffins rise and are nicely browned, they are done.

These muffins are a sensation at the breakfast table!

New Orleans Beignets

½ cup butter

1 t sugar

½ t salt

1 cup water

1 cup + 2T sifted, all-purpose flour

4 eggs

1 t vanilla

Oil for frying

4 X powdered sugar

Heat butter, sugar, salt, and water until it comes to a boil. Remove from heat and add flour, all at once. Stir until thoroughly mixed, and until mixture will leave sides of the pan. Add eggs, one at a time, and beat until smooth and glossy. Add vanilla and stir in. Heat oil (about 1½ inches deep) in electric frying pan with high sides. Drop heaping teaspoons of dough in oil, a few at the time. Brown on both sides. Drain and dust with 4 x sugar.

Light Buttermilk Pancakes

1 ½ cups flour

1 T sugar

1 t baking powder

½ t salt

3 egg yolks and three egg whites

1 2/3 cups buttermilk

1 t baking soda

3 T melted butter

Sift together flour, sugar, baking powder, and salt. Beat egg whites. Add soda to buttermilk, and stir into beaten egg yolks. Add liquids to dry ingredients. Stir in butter and fold in stiffly beaten egg whites. (If using self rising flour, omit baking powder and salt.) Bake on hot griddle.

Angel Yeast Waffles

2 cups milk	2 ½ cups self-rising flour
½ cup butter	1 t sugar
1 package dry yeast	2 eggs, separated
¼ cup water	1/8 t baking soda

Heat: milk and butter until butter melts. Cool mixture to lukewarm.

Dissolve: yeast in warm water. Add to milk mixture.

Stir: in flour and sugar until smooth.

Cover: and refrigerate overnight.

Heat: waffle iron.

Beat: egg yolks and soda into refrigerated batter.

Beat: egg whites to stiff peaks. Fold into batter leaving some white fluffs.

Pour: batter into hot waffle iron. Cook until steaming stops.

Makes: about 6 to 8 waffles.

For Dessert Waffles: Use 2 T sugar and 3 eggs. Serve with sweetened fruit and fresh whipped cream or ice cream.

Salads

Let first the onion flourish there
Rose among the roots, the maiden-fair
Wine-scented and poetic soul
Of the capacious salad bowl.
　　　　~from *To a Gardener*, by Robert Louis Stevenson

The way in which Robert Louis Stevenson idealizes the onion might suggest that he anticipated the Vidalia onion of this noble state of Georgia. To me, the Vidalia is better and sweeter than a purple onion or a spring onion.

Layered Green Salad

1 head iceberg lettuce
10 oz frozen green peas, raw
½ cup chopped celery
1 Vidalia onion, diced
1 can sliced water chestnuts
2 t sugar
1 ½ cups mayonnaise
Parmesan cheese

Break lettuce into bottom of oblong dish (13 X 16). Break frozen peas apart and spread on lettuce. To these greens add the layers of celery, onion, and water chestnuts. Sprinkle sugar over this mixture. Thin mayonnaise with a little milk or buttermilk—just until spreadable. Spread over all. Sprinkle generously with fresh parmesan cheese. Cover dish with plastic wrap and chill. (This is a good green salad for company because you can make it ahead of time.)

Broccoli Salad

2 bunches fresh broccoli florets   ½ large purple onion
1 ½ cups shredded cheddar cheese   ½ pound bacon

Toss bite-sized broccoli with cheese. Add chopped onion. (Nothing is better than a Vidalia, but the purple adds color to your salad.) Cook bacon and crumble into pieces. Mix together and add dressing:

1 cup mayonnaise, ½ cup sugar, and 3 T vinegar

Mix and toss into salad just before serving.

Lettuce Wedge Salad

When you are in a frantic hurry, and you must have a salad, cut a wedge of lettuce, sprinkle with your favorite salad dressing, and top with Parmesan cheese. Add a few diced tomatoes for color. Great to look at and great to eat!

Nancy Terrill's Pasta Salad

6 cups tri-colored pasta (makes 12 cups cooked)
1 cup ranch dressing
¾ cup barbecue sauce
½ cup bacon, cooked, cooled, and crumbled
½ cup chopped bell pepper
½ cup green onion, chopped,
½ cup red onion, chopped
½ cup cucumber or celery, chopped
Salt and pepper to taste

Cook pasta according to package directions and drain. Mix barbecue sauce and ranch dressing together. Set aside. To the pasta, add remaining ingredients. Then add the dressing. If you like, this salad may serve as a main dish.

Helen's Wild Rice and Cranberry Salad

This salad is most unusual and delicious and gives an unexpected flair to a dinner, whether served before the entrée or with the meal.

1 box Uncle Ben's long grain and wild rice
1 package dried cranberries
3 ribs of celery, chopped
4 green onions, chopped
2 oz jar of diced pimento
½ cup of Marzetti Cole Slaw Dressing
½ cup chopped cashews

Cook rice according to package directions and cool. Mix all other ingredients, and add rice.

Kim and Petey's Broccoli Cauliflower Salad

1 head broccoli, broken into small pieces
1 head cauliflower, broken into small pieces
½ cup sour cream
½ cup mayonnaise
1 package ranch dressing mix
½ cup canned garden peas, drained
Small bottle bacon bits
Grated cheddar cheese

Mix together sour cream, mayonnaise, and ranch dressing mix. Pour over the broken vegetables and stir. Sprinkle with bacon bits and grated cheese.

Asparagus Salad

¾ cup sugar	½ cup water
1 cup water	1 cup chopped celery
½ t salt	2 t grated onion
½ cup white vinegar	2 oz jar pimentos, drained
Juice of ½ lemon	½ cup chopped pecans
2 envelopes unflavored gelatin	1 can asparagus tips, drained

Mix sugar, water, salt, and vinegar, and bring to a boil. Add gelatin which has been softened in 1/2 cup cold water. When cool, add other ingredients and mold. (You may add English peas, avocado, water chestnuts, etc.)

Cucumber Salad

1 pack unflavored gelatin
¾ cup water
1-3 oz package lime Jello
1-8 oz pack cream cheese
1 small cucumber, grated
1 t prepared horseradish
¼ cup onion, grated

Dissolve Jello and gelatin in boiling water. Stir in softened cream cheese. Add all other ingredients. Mold and chill.

Shrimp Salad in Tomato Aspic Ring

<u>Cook</u>: desired amount of shrimp. Clean and chill. Cut into moderate size chunks. (If small, cut in half.)

<u>Add</u>: 1 cup celery hearts, (delicate in flavor), cut into fine pieces.

<u>Sprinkle</u>: with salt and pepper.

<u>Stir in</u>: 1/2 cup mayonnaise (Do not use too much mayonnaise. Stir in a little at a time until the mixture is pleasantly but not excessively dressed.)

<u>Serve</u> in center of tomato aspic ring.

Tomato Aspic

1 quart can tomatoes
Celery, as desired
1 small bottle stuffed olives, sliced
1 T salt
3 T vinegar

1/4 t cayenne pepper
1 T grated onion
1 envelope Knox gelatin
1/2 cup cold water

Mash tomatoes to pulp, removing any stem. Cut celery fine. Drain and slice olives and add. Add all seasonings. Put gelatin in cold water for 10 minutes. Then heat over boiling water. Add to tomato mixture. Turn into molds that have been rinsed in cold water. Place in ring mold and refrigerate until firm.

We always enjoyed shrimp salad at the beach. It was wonderful in the trailer on a hot day. We had to enjoy it without the aspic, because our refrigerator was an ice box!

Cucumber Ring

2 envelopes unflavored gelatin
¼ cup cold water
1-8 oz package cream cheese
2 cups cucumber, peeled, grated, drained
Juice of 1½ lemons

1 cup mayonnaise
¼ cup onion, chopped
¼ cup parsley, chopped
½ t salt

Soften gelatin in cold water. Dissolve over hot water in double boiler. In a separate bowl, stir cheese to soften. Add remaining ingredients. Mix well. Stir gelatin into cheese mixture. Pour into mold and chill until firm.

Green Bean Salad

1½ T oil

½ cup vinegar

½ cup sugar

Salt and pepper to taste

1 can French cut green beans

1 purple onion, cut in rings

1/3 cup bean juice

Drain beans, reserve juice. Place beans and onions in bowl. Mix oil, vinegar, and sugar together in saucepan and bring to boil. Pour vinegar mixture over beans and onions. Add bean juice and let stay in refrigerator 24 hours.

Pork and Bean Salad

Helen says this is great with fried fish!

1-53 oz pork and beans, drained

1 large onion, chopped

1 tomato, chopped

1 bell pepper, chopped

1 cup sugar

½ cup cider vinegar

Mix together, refrigerate for at least one hour then serve.

Potato Salad

5 pounds white Irish potatoes
1 small Vidalia onion, finely chopped
2 T prepared mustard
Salt and pepper
Durkees Spread to taste

1 cup pickle relish
2 T sugar
¼ pint mayonnaise
1 cup finely chopped celery

Cut potatoes into cubes, put in heavy pot, and boil in about 1 inch salt water for 15 minutes. Test the potatoes with a fork and let cool. Add all other ingredients, stir, and chill. Serve cold.

Perfection Salad

1 envelope unflavored gelatin
¼ cup cold water
¼ cup sugar
½ t salt
1 cup hot water
¼ cup mild vinegar

1 T lemon juice
2 oz jar diced pimento, drained
¾ cup finely shredded cabbage
¾ cup chopped celery
¼ cup grated carrots
Salad greens

Soften gelatin in cold water. Add sugar, salt, hot water, and stir until dissolved. Add vinegar and lemon juice. Cool. When gelatin begins to thicken, add vegetables. (You may add a few English peas, if you like.) Pour in molds and chill until firm. Unmold onto salad greens to serve.

Perfection salad was among the first congealed salads to be publicized when gelatin came into common use. It is delicious—sharp, tangy, and crisp. It will remind you of a very good slaw.

Coca-Cola Salad

1 can dark pitted cherries, sweet
1 small can crushed pineapple
1-3 oz package cherry Jello
1-3 oz pack strawberry Jello
1-8 oz pack cream cheese
2-6 oz Coca-Colas

Drain cherries and pineapple. Reserve liquid. Heat the liquid to boiling point, add Jello and stir until completely dissolved. Add softened cream cheese and mix thoroughly. Pour Cokes gently into mix. Pour into mold and refrigerate until set.

Pineapple and Carrot Salad

½ envelope unflavored gelatin
2 T water
1 (3-oz) package orange Jello
1 cup boiling water
1 cup grated carrots
½ cup mayonnaise
2 T lemon juice
1 small can crushed pineapple
¾ cup evaporated milk
Dash salt

In one bowl, soften gelatin in cold water; in another, dissolve Jello in hot water. Let cool while grating carrots. Combine carrots and mayonnaise and mix well. Add pineapple to gelatin mix, then the lemon juice, milk, and salt. Combine with the carrot and mayonnaise mixture. Mix well and mold.

Simple Cranberry Salad

2-3 oz packages strawberry Jello
2 cups hot water
2 cups sugar
1 pound cranberries, ground
2 oranges, ground, peel & all
½ cup chopped nuts

Dissolve Jello in hot water. Add sugar, stir in other ingredients. Mold and serve. This salad is an incredible addition to a turkey dinner.

Easy Holiday Cranberry Salad

2-3 oz packages raspberry Jello
2 cups boiling water
1-8 ½ oz can crushed pineapple
1 can whole cranberry sauce
1-8 oz package cream cheese
1 small carton sour cream
1 cup chopped nuts
½ t vanilla

Dissolve Jello in 2 cups boiling water. Stir in pineapple with juice. Fold in cranberry sauce and ½ cup chopped nuts. Place this mixture in a Pyrex dish and chill until set. Beat softened cream cheese and sour cream together with a hand mixer on low speed, and add vanilla and ¼ cup powdered sugar (optional). Spread over set mixture and sprinkle with remaining ½ cup chopped nuts.

Strawberry Salad

1-3 oz package strawberry Jello
1 envelope unflavored gelatin
2 cups boiling water
1-10 oz pack frozen strawberries
1 can crushed pineapple
1 cup chopped nuts

Add boiling water to Jello and gelatin. Stir in frozen strawberries. Add other ingredients, mold and serve.

Lime Jello Salad

1 (3-oz) package lime Jello
1 cup boiling water
1 cup miniature marshmallows
Small package cream cheese
½ cup chopped nuts
Small can crushed pineapple
3 t mayonnaise
½ pint whipped cream

Dissolve Jello in hot water. Add marshmallows. Soften cream cheese and cut into hot mixture. Stir until marshmallows dissolve. Chill until cold and thickening, then add nuts, pineapple, and mayonnaise. Fold in whipped cream and mold. (<u>This salad is a Christmas favorite</u>.)

Buttermilk Lime Salad

1-6 oz pack lime Jello
1 ½ cups boiling water
One large can crushed pineapple
1 cup buttermilk
1- 8 oz container cool whip
1 cup chopped nuts

Dissolve Jello in 1½ cups boiling water. Let cool. Add crushed pineapple and buttermilk. When slightly thickened, stir in cool whip and nuts. Refrigerate. This recipe is so easy, and a great substitute for the Lime Jello Salad above.

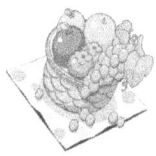

Easy Frozen Fruit Salad

1 can condensed milk
1 large can crushed pineapple
Chopped nuts, if desired
1 small carton cool whip
1 large can cherry pie filling

Stir all together and freeze.

Delicious! This is the one we always use if we are in a hurry.

Six Cup Salad

1 cup mandarin orange sections
1 cup pineapple chunks, drained
1 cup miniature marshmallows
1 cup grated coconut
1 cup sour cream
1 cup fruit cocktail, drained

Mix all ingredients, chill, and serve as a salad or a dessert.

Cole Slaw

1 small head green cabbage	Marzetti slaw dressing
1 T salt	

Cut cabbage into four parts; then sliver thin strips by cutting across the leaves with a sharp knife. You should have four to six cups of cut cabbage. Sprinkle with salt, toss, and cover. Place in refrigerator for one hour. Remove cabbage from the refrigerator and drain, add Marzetti dressing. Toss and serve. Do not put too much dressing, but just enough to make the slaw glossy.

Waldorf Salad

Sometimes, we forget how delicious a traditional, simple recipe can be. Waldorf salad is a good example of an often forgotten but unusually satisfying addition to a meal.

2 cups chopped apples	½ cup chopped nuts
2 ribs celery	Mayonnaise to taste
2 T fresh orange juice	

Chop up apples, leaving peeling on fruit. Stir in orange juice. Chop celery fine, and add to apples. Add chopped nuts and stir. Stir in mayonnaise, beginning with ¼ cup. Add more if necessary. (Dress lightly for best flavor and effect.)

Waldorf Salad Variation

2 cups chopped apples
2 bananas
(raisins optional)

½ cup chopped nuts
Mayonnaise to taste

Blend all above ingredients. If raisins are used, golden are best. The darker raisins will darken the salad.

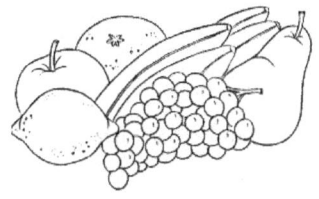

Grape Salad

5 pounds seedless grapes, red & green
1 cup sour cream
¾ cup light brown sugar

8 oz cream cheese
1 cup granulated sugar
1 cup chopped toasted pecans

In a large bowl mix together softened cream cheese, sour cream and granulated sugar. Add grapes and fold until grapes are well coated. Pour into a 9x13 Pyrex dish. Sprinkle brown sugar over grapes then top with nuts. Refrigerate.

Debbie's Potato Salad

5 lbs red potatoes
1 cup oil
½ cup vinegar
2 T sugar
Salt and pepper, to taste
1 cup chopped celery
1 cup chopped onion
1 cup chopped green pepper
Honey mustard dressing
Mayonnaise

Cut up, but do not peel, potatoes and boil until tender, drain. Mix oil, vinegar, sugar, salt and pepper. Pour over warm potatoes. Refrigerate overnight. Before serving add chopped vegetables and toss with dressing and mayonnaise (about ¼ cup each).

Greek Shrimp Pasta Salad

8 oz tri-colored rotini pasta, cooked as directed on package
1/3 cup lemon juice
3 T mayonnaise
1 single serve packet Splenda
1 pound peeled, cooked shrimp
¼ cup chopped red onion
1 small can black olives, drained
1 T Greek seasoning
½ t minced garlic
¼ cup olive oil
1 cup chopped tomatoes
2 T parsley
Feta cheese

Whisk together lemon juice, Greek seasoning, mayo, garlic and Splenda. Gradually add olive oil. Cover and chill. Combine cooked pasta, shrimp, tomatoes, onions, olives, and parsley. Drizzle with dressing, tossing to coat. Chill at least 1 hour. Crumble feta cheese on top when ready to eat.

Dorito Salad

6 cups mixed salad greens	1-15 oz can chili beans, mild
1 small red onion, sliced	1 large tomato, diced
1 small can sliced black olives	2 cups shredded cheddar cheese
1 large bag original flavor Doritos	1 bottle Catalina French dressing

This salad is best prepared just before ready to serve. Do not drain chili beans. Mix tomatoes, chili beans, and Catalina dressing together and chill. Crush Doritos into large bite size pieces. Drain black olives. When ready to serve mix all ingredients together.

Soups, Casseroles, and Main Dishes

"It's an ill cook that cannot lick his own fingers."
~from *Romeo and Juliet*, by William Shakespeare

The tasting that goes on in a good kitchen is sublime! A soup pot or main dish, especially, is sampled again and again as it simmers away on the stove. That's part of what a kitchen is all about.

Soups

"One small serving of a ravishing soup is infuriating. It is like seeing the Pearly Gates swing shut in one's face after one brief glimpse of Heaven."
~from *Cross Creek Cookery,* by Marjorie Kinnan Rawlings

Potato Soup

Six large potatoes, cubed	Salt and pepper to taste
1 cup carrots, sliced	¼ cup all purpose flour
1 quart chicken broth (2 cans)	2 cups half and half
2 celery ribs, thinly sliced	1 t fresh basil or chives
1 medium onion, diced	

Place cubed potatoes in a heavy pot with a good-fitting lid. Add the carrots, broth, celery, onion, and seasonings. Cook until vegetables are tender. Stir together the flour and the half and half and add to the soup. Add herbs and heat through, stirring gently. Serve with hot corn bread.

Cream of Broccoli Soup

1 can chicken broth	¼ t celery salt
½ cup chopped onion	¼ t white pepper
2 cups cut fresh broccoli	1/8 t garlic salt
2 T butter	1 ½ cups half and half
3 T all purpose flour	Fresh parsley

Combine first three ingredients in saucepan. Bring mixture to a boil. Reduce heat. Cover and simmer for 10 minutes, or until broccoli is tender. Cool slightly. Place vegetable mixture in food processor. Cover and blend for 30-60 seconds, until smooth. Set aside.

In same saucepan you used for the broccoli mixture, melt butter. Blend in flour, celery salt, pepper, and garlic salt. Add half and half. Cook and stir until mixture is thickened. (Heat thoroughly, but do not boil.) Stir in broccoli mixture. Cook and stir until soup is heated through. Serves 6. Double to serve 12. Spoon soup into bowls, and garnish center of bowl with a light sprig of the parsley.

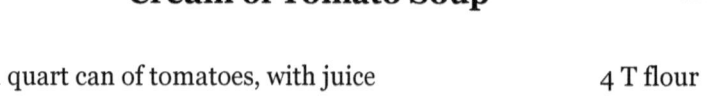

Cream of Tomato Soup

1 quart can of tomatoes, with juice	4 T flour
1 slice onion	1 quart milk
4 T butter	¾ t baking soda

Boil tomatoes until tender (15 minutes). To this add the onion. When the onion is done and its flavors have seeped into the soup, remove it from soup pot and discard. Place tomatoes in food processor and blend well. Set aside. In same soup pot, melt butter, stir in flour, salt and pepper, and add milk. Stir until thickened and scalding. Add the soda to the tomato mixture, and pour this mixture into your soup pot. Heat through.

Chicken Casserole

It is not surprising that our favorite casseroles are chicken! "Chicken every Sunday" was the idea of gourmet cooking when we were growing up. The Chicken Casserole below is my favorite. Helen's favorite follows.

4 slices day old bread, cubed	1/2 t salt
2 cups diced cooked chicken	1/4 t pepper
1/4 cup diced celery	2 eggs
1/4 cup diced onion	2 cups milk, divided
1/4 cup diced green pepper	1 can cream of mushroom soup
1/4 cup mayonnaise	1/2 cup grated cheese

Place two slices cubed bread in greased casserole. Combine chicken, celery, onion, green pepper, mayonnaise, salt, and pepper. Pour over bread crumbs. Top with remaining cubes of bread. Beat eggs and 1½ cups milk; pour over top. Refrigerate overnight. When ready to cook, sprinkle cheese over top of casserole. Combine soup and ½ cup milk; pour over mixture. Bake at 350° for one hour.

Chicken Salad Casserole

4 cups cooked chicken, diced	1 cup mayonnaise
1 cup celery, diced	1 cup chopped pecans
2 oz jar diced pimento, drained	1 T diced onion
2 cans cream of chicken soup	2 t lemon juice
½ t salt, dash pepper	2 cups potato chips, crushed

Mix all ingredients except potato chips, and pour into a greased 3 quart, flat casserole dish. Bake at 350° for 20 minutes. Top casserole with crushed chips, and return to the oven just to heat.

Chicken and Dumplings

Chicken

Cook a chicken on top of stove in a big pot, with plenty of liquid. (Cooking requires at least an hour; chicken should be tender.) Remove chicken from pot, and debone. Set aside.

Dumplings

1 egg, beaten	1/2 cup hot water
1 t oil	Self-rising flour

Beat egg, add oil and hot water, then gradually add the flour to form dough. Begin with two cups, and add more if needed to make a biscuit-like dough. Knead lightly and roll out (thin) on pastry cloth. Cover with a cloth and let stand at least one hour, (three is better!). Cut into strips and cook as follows:

Drop into lightly boiling (simmering) chicken broth, a few pieces at the time, keeping the broth at the same temperature, until all dumplings are in. Cover and cook until done. Helen is the expert, and sometimes gives a lucky relative frozen dumplings for Christmas!

Chicken with Sour Cream and Bacon

1 package chipped beef	1 cup sour cream
2 slices bacon, cut in half lengthwise	1 can mushroom soup
4 boneless chicken breasts	

Line a baking pan with chipped beef. Wrap each chicken breast with bacon, and place on the beef. Combine the mushroom soup and sour cream, and pour over all. Cook uncovered one hour at 300°; then cover and cook another 30 minutes.

Dinner in a Dish

1 T olive oil	¼ t pepper
1 medium sized onion	2 eggs
2 green peppers, sliced	2 cups fresh or frozen corn
1 pound ground beef	4 medium tomatoes, sliced
½ t salt	½ cup dry bread crumbs

Put oil in skillet and lightly fry onions and peppers for three minutes. Add meat and blend thoroughly. Continue cooking until hamburger is done. Add seasoning. Remove from heat, stir in eggs, and mix well. Put one cup of the corn in baking dish, then half of the meat mixture, then a layer of corn, meat mixture, and sliced tomatoes. Cover with bread crumbs. Dot with butter. Bake in 350° oven for 40 minutes.

My mother got this recipe at a cooking school in the 1930's. We loved it!

Scalloped Oysters

1 quart select oysters	1/2 cup buttered bread crumbs
2 cups of oyster crackers	3 T butter, melted
1 egg	Salt and pepper to taste
1/2 cup milk	

Remove any pieces of shell from oysters, warm, but do not cook. Drain in colander. In a baking pan, from which they are to be served, put a layer of oysters, salt, pepper, and bits of butter, then a layer of crushed crackers (having them not too fine). Continue until all are used, having oysters on the top. Break egg into the milk and whisk. Pour egg and milk mix over oysters. In separate bowl, combine butter and crumbs. Sprinkle over casserole. Bake in a 325° degree oven about 30 minutes or until the oysters and egg are cooked. Serve at once.

Barbecued Pork Chops

Place 4 to 6 pork chops in a greased baking dish and make a sauce as follows, pouring over the chops.

3 T brown sugar	2 T vinegar
1 cup catsup	Dash paprika
2 T Worcestershire sauce	1 lemon
1/2 cup prepared barbecue sauce	Dash salt

Cover chops with sauce; fit foil over baking pan. Bake at 350° for one hour, and uncover for the last 15 minutes. Cook longer if chops are very thick.

Gumbo

<u>Brown in large skillet</u>: 1 pound ground beef; drain off liquid.
<u>Add</u>: 1 medium onion, 2 cans tomatoes, and 2 cups fresh or frozen okra.
<u>Season with</u>: salt and pepper.
<u>Cook and simmer:</u> one hour. <u>Serve</u>: over rice.

Sunday Roast Beef

<u>Place in pan</u>: Eye of round roast
<u>Mix</u>: 1 can golden mushroom soup
    1 package dry onion soup
    1/4 cup Worcestershire sauce and 1/2 cup water
<u>Pour</u>:   liquid over roast.
<u>Cover</u>: with foil.
<u>Cook</u>: two hours at 350°.
<u>Slice roast</u> and arrange on platter. Serve gravy in bowl.

Beef Stroganoff

2 onions, chopped	1 t Worcestershire sauce
3 T butter	Salt and pepper
2 T flour	1 1/2 pounds sirloin, cut in strips
1 cup stock or consommé	1/2 pound mushrooms
1 T tomato paste or catsup	1 cup sour cream and sherry

Saute onions in butter until transparent. Stir in flour, add other liquid. Cook and stir until smooth and thick. In an iron skillet or heavy fry pan, saute beef strips until lightly browned. Saute mushrooms in same pan, adding more butter if necessary. Combine beef strips and mushrooms with sauce. Add salt and pepper and stir in sour cream and ½ cup sherry. Heat to boiling but do not boil.

Party Beef Dinner

2 pounds ground beef	3/4 cup liquid (mushroom juice and water)
2 T oil	
1 cup chopped onion	1 can tomatoes
1 cup chopped green pepper	2 t salt
1 cup chopped celery	½ t pepper
1 can (4 oz) mushrooms, drained	¾ cup rice

In a large, heavy pot or skillet, brown beef in oil. Pour off drippings, and then add other ingredients. Cover tightly, simmering until rice is done, about 45 minutes. Stir occasionally. **(This is another great cooking school dish.)**

Cranberry Chicken

6 boneless chicken breasts
1 can whole cranberry sauce

1-8 oz jar French dressing
1 package onion soup mix

Place a small amount of oil in an electric frying pan and brown chicken pieces lightly on both sides. Place the browned chicken in a Pyrex baking dish 9 x 13 inches in size. Combine the last three ingredients and pour over chicken. Cover baking pan with foil. Cook for about 1 hour at 350°, or until chicken is tender. Breasts with the bone in may be used, but cooking time should be increased to an hour and a half.

Easy Baked Chicken

2 or 3 small fryers, quartered (chicken breasts or thighs may be used instead)
Salt and pepper
1 package dry onion soup mix
1 small bottle Wishbone Italian dressing
Several lemons

Place washed chicken pieces in casserole dish that has been sprayed with Pam. Add salt and pepper to taste. (Little salt will be needed.) In small bowl, combine Italian dressing and soup mix. Pour over chicken. Slice lemons thinly and place over chicken. Cover dish with foil and place in refrigerator overnight. Before cooking, remove some of the lemon slices, depending upon lemon taste desired. Bake covered in 350° oven for one hour. Remove foil, bake 30 minutes more.

Fried Chicken

Every Southern cook needs to know how to fry a chicken. It is not hard if you have a deep fryer.

Select a couple of fryers weighing from 1 and a half to 2 pounds.

<u>Cut</u> up the fryer, or if you don't know how, have the butcher prepare it.

When you are ready to fry:

<u>Pour oil</u> into fryer to the level suggested for deep frying.

<u>Set fryer</u> temperature (about 375º).

<u>Wash and skin</u> chickens, pat dry, and sprinkle with salt and pepper.

      (Soak dark pieces for a while in cold water.)

<u>Sift</u> about a cup of all-purpose flour into a baking dish.

<u>Dip</u> chicken pieces into flour. Coat thoroughly.

<u>Drop</u> pieces into the fry basket and lower into the oil, according to the directions on your deep fryer.

<u>Do not</u> try to cook too much chicken at one time.

<u>Fry</u> at about 375º. It takes 12-13 minutes for the white meat, and about 15 minutes for the dark. Fry until chicken is brown

and floats on top.

<u>Drain</u> on paper towels over newspapers.

ARRANGE CHICKEN ATTRACTIVELY ON A PLATE. BE PROUD.

Standing Rib Roast

Salt a standing rib roast. Cook in moderate oven at 350°, uncovered, fat side up:

    18-20 minutes to the pound for rare roast,
    22-25 for medium,
    27-30 for well done.

Sunday Pot Roast

    1 good beef roast, 3 ½ to 4 pounds
    4 Vidalia onions, or use white or yellow ones
    1 large bag carrots
    1 ½ pounds small red potatoes (new potatoes)
    Worcestershire sauce (about a third of a cup)
    Salt and pepper to taste

You may select a rump, sirloin, or round roast. Rump slices especially well, yet cooks up to be a tender roast. In a Dutch oven or deep cooking pot, brown the roast on all sides in some oil or bacon drippings. When the roast is browned all over, remove from the pan and discard drippings. Do not wash pot. Replace roast in pot, salt well. Turn pan on high. As roast begins to sizzle, place the vegetables around it, and sprinkle the roast with the Worcestershire sauce. Add ¼ cup water, and place lid on the pot quickly to prevent steam from escaping. Lower heat, cover, and simmer for three hours, or until you get home from church.

Family Baked Chicken

6 boned chicken breasts
1 package dry onion soup
1 can mushroom soup
½ cup milk

Place chicken breasts in greased casserole dish. Do not overlap. Sprinkle onion soup on top. Cover with mushroom soup, which has been thinned with the milk. Cover with foil, and bake 1 hour at 350°. If unboned chicken breasts are used, increase baking time to 1 ½ hours. To brown, remove foil for last ten minutes.

Stuffed Shrimp

2 pounds jumbo shrimp
3 T butter
2 T minced green onion
1 green pepper, chopped
1 cup soft bread crumbs
1 t salt, 1/8 t pepper
1 egg, beaten
2 T melted butter

Shell and devein six shrimp. (Set rest aside.) Cook these 6 shrimp in 2 T melted butter for two minutes or until pink. Remove these to cutting board. Sauté onions and peppers for four minutes. Stir in crumbs. Chop the six shrimp, add salt, pepper, chopped shrimp, and egg. Shell remaining shrimp, leaving tails on. Place shrimp on cutting board, and slit along underneath with knife. (Don't cut through.) Mound stuffing in each shrimp. Place shrimp (tail up) in a greased baking dish. Cook, or refrigerate until ready to cook. Drizzle shrimp with melted butter. Bake 12 minutes at 350° degrees. Transfer to warm platter. Garnish with parsley.

Boiled Shrimp

Boil 4 quarts of water in a large pot. Add crab boil and salt, or you may use celery leaves and red pepper. Use a little vinegar to lessen cooking odors. Add the shrimp and return to a full rolling boil. Take off heat and let stand in water for 3 minutes for mediums and 5 minutes for jumbos. Shell, devein, chill, and serve with saltines and cocktail sauce.

Shrimp Casserole with Green Noodles

2 pounds shrimp	Dash of salt and pepper
10 oz green noodles	1 cup mayonnaise
8 oz mushrooms	8 oz sour cream
½ cup butter	1 T chopped chives
1 can cream of mushroom soup	4 T dry sherry

Cook, clean, and devein shrimp or buy it frozen and ready to use. Cook noodles and drain. Set these aside. Blend other ingredients and simmer in a saucepan, heating well. Layer noodles, shrimp, and sauce. Bake at 350° for 45 minutes.

Shrimp Casserole

3 cups shrimp, cooked and deveined	1 T Worcestershire Sauce
1 cup mayonnaise	1 package ranch dressing
2 cups cooked rice (Uncle Ben's)	1 can mushrooms, drained
1 T grated onion	3 T butter (melted)
1 small can LeSueur peas & juice	Pepper to taste
¼ cup cooking sherry	Buttered bread crumbs

Mix all ingredients and top with buttered bread crumbs. Bake at 350° for 30 minutes. Serves 8. Recipe may be doubled for fifteen.

This casserole was a favorite with the families at the beach.

Shrimp Creole

<u>Clean and devein:</u> a pound (or a pound and a half) of raw shrimp. Do not cook. (If you have fresh shrimp that have been cooked and chilled you may use them instead if you do not simmer too long.)

<u>Cook all together on top of stove</u>:

1 T oil	1 clove garlic minced
1 cup diced celery	3 T flour
1 cup diced onion	2 cans tomatoes
1 cup diced green pepper	½ cup catsup
1 T Worcestershire	Pinch of sugar & salt

<u>Add</u>: Raw Shrimp, fresh or frozen and thawed.

<u>Cook</u>: About 10 minutes, until raw shrimp are done. Serve over rice.

Deviled Crab

2 T butter	1 t salt
2 T flour	1 T chopped parsley
1 cup milk	2 boiled eggs, chopped
2 t lemon juice	½ t horseradish
1 t prepared mustard	½ cup bread crumbs
1 can crab meat, or 1 cup fresh	6 crab shells

Melt butter in sauce pan, add flour, and stir until blended. Add milk gradually, stirring until smooth and thick, and then add remaining ingredients. Mix well, and put in crab shells or individual shell dishes. Sprinkle with bread crumbs. Bake at 400° for 15 minutes.

Down Home Meat Loaf

2 pounds ground beef
2 eggs
1 ½ cups bread crumbs or oatmeal
¾ cup catsup

1 T Worcestershire sauce
¼ cup Italian dressing
½ cup warm water
1 pack dry onion soup mix

Mix all ingredients thoroughly. Shape into a loaf and place in a greased baking pan. Bake for one hour at 350°.

Chicken Pot Pie

4 cups cooked, chopped chicken
1-16 oz package frozen mixed veggies
1 stick melted butter
1 cup milk

1 can cream of celery soup
1 can cream of chicken soup
1 can chicken broth

Mix all ingredients. Pour into a 12 X 18 flat casserole dish that has been sprayed with Pam. Top with thin-cut biscuits.

See the bread section for biscuit recipe. You may roll out biscuit dough, then cut into biscuits, and place the biscuits on the casserole. Bake at 350° for 25 to 35 minutes, or until biscuits are nicely browned and casserole is bubbly.

Aunt Mae's Plum Sauce

Boil ½ gallon of ripe plums for 5 minutes, in just enough water to cover. Pour off the water, and save it to make plum jelly. Add 6 cups of sugar, and 1 teaspoon each cloves, allspice, and cinnamon. Add 1 pint vinegar to cooked plums. Boil gently for 30-40 minutes, stirring constantly. Pour into jars and seal. This sauce is delicious with any meat: chicken, pork, beef, or turkey.

Zesty Gold Corn Chili

2 lbs ground beef
1 large onion, diced
2 packages mild chili seasoning mix
1-15 oz can light red kidney beans
2-14 oz cans diced tomatoes with onion and garlic
1-7 oz can diced green chilies, drained (optional)
1-15 oz can black beans
1 large can whole kernel corn

Brown meat, add onions and cook until tender. Drain beans and corn. Add the remaining ingredients and simmer for about 2 hours.

Chicken Enchiladas

3 or 4 boneless chicken breasts
8 oz sour cream
1 can cream of chicken soup
1 can Rotel tomatoes
¾ cup shredded cheese
Flour tortillas

Grill chicken and cut into bite size pieces. In a saucepan mix sour cream, soup, and tomatoes and simmer until heated through. Add chicken. Fill tortillas and roll up. Place tortillas in a 9x13 greased baking dish. Sprinkle shredded cheese over top. Bake for 25 minutes at 350°.

Another option: Brown chicken, add 1-8 oz pack of cream cheese, the soup, tomatoes, and cheese. Place all in crockpot early in the morning and cook on low to be ready at supper. Serve with flour tortillas and sour cream.

Beach Shrimp

3 lbs frozen, peeled, jumbo raw shrimp, thawed
1-16 oz bottle Italian dressing
2 garlic cloves, finely chopped
¼ cup chopped parsley
1 1/2 T ground pepper
2 lemons, halved
1 stick butter, cut in pieces

Place first 4 ingredients in a 13x9 casserole dish, tossing to coat. Squeeze lemons over shrimp mixture and stir. Add lemon halves to dish. Sprinkle evenly with parsley, dot with butter. Bake at 375° for 25 minutes, stirring after 15 minutes.

Serve with crusty French bread to "mop" the sauce and a green salad. Wonderful!

Easy Chicken Pie

Boil a fryer until tender and cut into bite-sized pieces. Mix with:
- 4 chopped boiled eggs
- 1 can cream of mushroom soup

Put in a greased 9x13 casserole dish.

Mix together:
- 1 ½ cups chicken broth
- ½ cup mayonnaise

Pour over chicken. **DO NOT STIR.**

Mix together:
- 1 stick melted butter
- 1 cup flour
- 1 cup milk

Pour over top. **DO NOT STIR.** Bake at 350° for 1 hour until golden brown.

Crock Pot 3 Cheese Tortellini with Spinach

1 large package refrigerated 3 cheese tortellini
4 cups chicken broth
2-14 oz cans petite diced tomatoes
1-8oz package cream cheese, softened
1 T dried oregano
1 T dried basil
4 cups fresh spinach

Combine all ingredients in crock pot. Stir gently. Cover and cook on low for 6 hours. Serve with garlic bread and a green salad.

Miracle Pasta

1-12 oz package linguine pasta, uncooked, broken in half
1 (28 oz) can diced tomatoes
4 cloves garlic, thinly sliced
2 t dried oregano
½ t salt
2 T chopped fresh basil
1 onion, cut in julienne strips
4 ½ cups chicken broth
½ t crushed red pepper flakes
2 T olive oil
Grated Parmesan cheese

In a soup pot, place linguine, tomatoes, onion, and garlic. Pour in chicken broth and sprinkle with oregano, crushed red pepper, and salt. Drizzle top with oil and cover.

Bring to a boil over medium heat, reduce heat to low, and simmer 10 minutes, stirring every 2 to 3 minutes, or until liquid is almost gone. Stir in basil and serve garnished with Parmesan cheese.

What makes this dish a miracle is the fact that it couldn't be any easier to make! You can prepare and serve this pasta dish in just 20 minutes. Put everything in one pot, cover, cook, and you've got a delicious dinner ready! To complete it, add a green salad and slices of garlic bread.

Vegetable Dishes

"Human beings, vegetables, or cosmic dust—we all dance to a mysterious tune, intoned in the distance by an invisible piper."
        Albert Einstein, in *The Saturday Evening Post*, 26 October 1929

Fresh Corn Pudding

2 cups fresh corn cut from cob
1 T sugar
1 ½ t salt, dash pepper

3 eggs, lightly beaten
2 T butter
2 cups milk

Combine corn, sugar, salt, and black pepper. Add eggs and mix well. Add butter to milk and heat until butter is melted. Blend with the corn and egg mixtures. Turn into a buttered 1 quart casserole. Place in a pan of hot water. Bake in a preheated slow oven (325°) 1 hour or until knife inserted in the center comes out clean. When fresh corn is not in season, use frozen corn.

Squash Soufflé

Cook two cups of squash, pour into large mixing bowl, and mash to a pulp. Add the following:

1 cup breadcrumbs
1 cup milk
3 T butter, melted
1 cup grated cheese

3 or 4 eggs, beaten
Salt and pepper to taste
1 scant T sugar

Mix together the squash, breadcrumbs, milk, butter, grated cheese, beaten eggs, and seasonings. Beat until blended. Bake at 350° until set. If rushed, you may steam the squash, add salt and pepper, cover with a white sauce, and sprinkle with paprika. This dish will be an attractive platter to take to the table.

Spinach Soufflé

1 ½ T butter

1 ½ T flour

½ cup milk

2 cups cooked chopped spinach

1 T parmesan cheese

½ cup mayonnaise

3 eggs, well beaten

1 clove garlic, crushed

Salt to taste

Make a white sauce of butter, flour, and milk. Add other ingredients. Pour into greased casserole and bake at 350° for 30-45 minutes, until set.

Glazed Carrots

5 medium carrots, peeled and cut

1/4 cup butter

1/2 cup sugar

1/4 cup water

Make a syrup of butter, sugar, and water and pour over carrots. Bake at 375° until carrots are tender.

Sweet Potato Soufflé

3 cups cooked, mashed sweet potatoes

½ t nutmeg

¾ cup sugar

3 T butter, melted

1 cup milk

1 t cinnamon

3 eggs, separated

½ cup raisins (if desired)

½ cup chopped pecans (if desired)

Marshmallows

Beat the potatoes in an electric mixer. When potatoes are smooth, add the sugar, melted butter, milk, spices, and egg yolks. Beat egg whites until soft peaks form, fold into potato mixture. Pour into casserole dish and bake at 350° until set, about 35 minutes, then top with marshmallows and bake until lightly brown.

Broccoli Casserole

4 cups cooked broccoli, chopped	1 cup diced celery
1-10½ oz can cream of mushroom soup	½ t pepper
1 -2 oz jar sliced pimentos, drained	1 t salt
¾ cup sour cream	½ cup grated cheddar

In large mixing bowl, combine all ingredients except the cheese. Place in large oiled casserole and top with the cheddar cheese. Bake in 350° oven for 20-25 minutes.

Vidalia Onion Pie

1 cup crushed saltine or Ritz crackers	¼ cup melted butter

<u>Combine</u> the above ingredients and press into a 9" pie plate.

2 ½ cups thinly sliced Vidalia Onions	2 eggs
2 T butter	¾ cup milk
Salt and pepper	1 cup grated sharp cheese

Sauté onions in butter, then place in prepared pie plate. Combine the eggs and milk and pour over onions in the pie plate. Sprinkle lightly with salt and pepper, and then top with cheese. Bake for 45 minutes at 350°.

Fried Onions

3 large onions 1 egg
1 cup flour 1 cup milk

Peel and slice onions. Separate into rings. Place onions in cold water for 30 minutes to an hour. Drain. Beat egg well and add milk. Dip rings into milk mixture, then into flour. Fry in hot oil until brown.

Stuffed Tomatoes

<u>Six medium tomatoes</u>
Filling:
    1 T salad or olive oil 1 t salt
    1 small onion, sliced 2 eggs
1 can (6 oz) chopped mushrooms, drained
1/2 cup sour cream
1 t dried tarragon leaves 1/4 t black pepper

Cut a thin, horizontal slice from stem end of each tomato. Carefully hollow out tomatoes. Place tomatoes in shallow baking dish. In hot oil, in medium skillet, sauté onion until tender. Add mushrooms, tarragon, and salt, and cook, stirring, for 5 minutes. In bowl whisk together eggs, sour cream, and pepper, just until combined. Stir in mushroom mixture. Use to fill tomatoes. Bake at 350° for 30-35 minutes, until the mixture inside the tomato is firmly set, like custard.

Horseradish Carrots

1 ½ pounds sliced carrots or baby carrots
1 cup mayonnaise
1 T grated onion
1 T prepared horseradish
¼ cup cheddar cheese, grated
1 cup buttered bread crumbs

Cook carrots in water until tender. Drain, saving ¼ cup of the cooking liquid. Mix liquid, mayonnaise, onion, and horseradish; add grated cheese. Pour this mixture over the carrots. Place in a prepared 1 ½ quart baking dish. Sprinkle buttered bread crumbs over all. (We use about 2 T butter.) Bake uncovered for 30 minutes at 350°.

Cabbage Casserole

1 small cabbage, shredded
1 medium onion, chopped
½ cup butter
¼ cup mayonnaise
1 can cream of mushroom
or cream of chicken soup

Spread cabbage in a flat 3 quart baking dish, which has been sprayed with Pam. Sprinkle onion on top. Melt butter and pour over cabbage. Sprinkle lightly with salt and pepper. Mix soup and mayonnaise, and spread over cabbage.

Topping: 1 stack pack of Ritz crackers
1 cup grated, sharp cheddar
1 stick butter, melted

Crush crackers in a gallon zip-lock bag, or crush in food processor. Add cheese and butter to crackers and mix well. Sprinkle over casserole, and bake 45 minutes at 350°.

Aunt Miriam's Vegetable Casserole

1 can shoepeg corn, drained
1 can French cut green beans, drained
½ cup grated sharp cheese
½ cup chopped onions
½ cup chopped green pepper
½ cup chopped celery
1 cup sour cream
1 can cream of celery soup

Mix all ingredients and place in prepared casserole dish.

Topping:
1 stack pack Ritz crackers, crushed
½ stick butter, melted

Mix and spread on top of casserole. Bake for 30 minutes at 350°.

Brown Rice

2 T butter
1 cup uncooked rice
1/3 cup sliced canned mushrooms
1 can onion soup
1 soup can water

Brown rice lightly in butter. Pour into baking dish with mushrooms, soup, and water. Bake at 375° for 25 minutes, or until liquid is absorbed.

Tomato Pie

Make a pie crust as instructed in bread and pastry section. Freeze the crust. When ready to prepare pie, prick the crust and bake at 400° until lightly browned.

Peel and slice four tomatoes and sprinkle with salt. Let drain 10 minutes. Place a layer of tomatoes in crust, and then sprinkle with chopped green onion and basil. Repeat for three layers. Mix one cup mayonnaise, 1 cup shredded sharp cheddar, and 1 cup shredded mozzarella cheese. Spread over filling. Bake for 30 minutes at 350°. This pie is great at breakfast, dinner, or supper.

Cakes, Pies, and Desserts

Mrs. Cratchit left the room alone—too nervous to bear witnesses—to take the pudding up, and bring it in. Suppose it should not be done enough! Suppose it should break in turning out! Suppose somebody should have got over the wall of the back-yard, and stolen it, while they were merry with the goose!

Hallo! A great deal of steam! The pudding was out of the copper. A smell like a washing day! That was the cloth. A smell like an eating-house and a pastry cook's next door to each other. That was the pudding. In half a minute Mrs. Cratchit entered: flushed, but smiling proudly: with the pudding, like a speckled cannon-ball, so hard and firm, blazing in half of half-a-quarter of ignited brandy, and bedight with Christmas holly stuck into the top.

~from *A Christmas Carol*, by Charles Dickens

Mrs. Bob Cratchit was a fine cook, who, "brave in ribbons," knew how to make a special day a real occasion, even on a tight budget. Her celebrated Christmas Pudding, described above, is similar to our fruit cakes. Helen's "Stir Fruitcake" is a good modern substitute for Mrs. Cratchit's creation. Our families, to tell the truth, prefer other cakes at holidays. The basic recipe for most of Helen's layer cakes, and mine, is the most versatile cake recipe we have ever tried. It never fails to please and make us proud!

1-2-3-4 Cake

1 cup Crisco	4 eggs
2 cups sugar	1 scant cup milk or 1 ½ cups buttermilk
3 cups self-rising flour~	1 t baking soda, if you use buttermilk
(We prefer White Lily)	1 t vanilla

Have shortening and eggs at room temperature. Cream Crisco and sugar until light and fluffy. Add eggs one at a time, blending in each. Add milk alternately with flour. (If you use buttermilk, sift the soda and flour together.) Add vanilla.

Have your cake pans ready, generously greased and floured. Measure batter into cake pans. If you have only one oven, bake your layers in shifts. Bake at 350° for about 12-15 minutes for five thinner layers, 18-20 minutes for four thicker layers.

<u>This recipe also makes a delicious plain cake, cooked in a tube or bundt pan.</u> If you want a plain cake to serve with pudding or sauce, use the following version:

1 cup butter	4 eggs, separated
2 cups sugar	1 scant cup milk
3 cups plain (all-purpose) flour	2 t baking powder, sifted with flour
	1 t vanilla

Mix this cake as described above, except beat egg whites separately, and fold into finished batter. Bake in a greased and floured tube pan at 350° for one hour.

Lemon Cheese Cake Filling

3 eggs	Grated rind 1 lemon
½ cup hot water	Juice of 2 lemons
1 ¾ cups sugar	1 peeled grated apple
1 T flour mixed with sugar	1 T butter

To have plenty of filling, you may use this icing recipe.

5 eggs	Grated rind 2 lemons
¾ cups hot water	Juice of 3 lemons
2 and 1/3 cups sugar	1 large grated apple
2 T flour mixed with sugar	1 ½ T butter

Beat eggs well and pour in hot water gradually. Add sugar, which has been mixed with flour. Next add rind, lemon juice, grated apple, and butter. Cook in double boiler to a jelly (takes about 45 minutes) and let cool. After it is cool and thick, spread on cake. Spread very thin so that you will have enough for all five layers. Place between layers and on top and sides of 1-2-3-4- cake.

This cake is a favorite in my family, and we bake it often. It is high, light, and deliciously lemony. Helen's family's favorite in former days was a 12-layer chocolate, until she discovered Italian Cream. Yummy! First Place!

If you are short of time and a birthday looms, make 4 or 5 nice layers of a 1-2-3-4 cake. Fill and cover with **a butter cream frosting**: <u>1 stick butter, three cups powdered sugar, 1/3 cup half and half, and a teaspoon of vanilla</u>. Beat until creamy and spread on layers. You may add more powdered sugar or more liquid to get the consistency you wish. Remember, the terms *icing, frosting,* and *filling* are used interchangeably in this recipe book.

Stir Fruit Cake

2 sticks soft butter	1 cup self-rising flour
1 cup sugar	1 quart chopped pecans
4 eggs	2 t vanilla flavoring

¼ to ½ pound candied cherries, chopped
2 t orange or lemon flavoring
¼ to ½ pound candied pineapple, chopped
2 t almond flavoring
1 small bag orange slice candy, chopped   2 t pumpkin pie spice

Cream butter and sugar together until light and fluffy. Add eggs, one at a time. In a separate bowl, sprinkle flour over the fruits and nuts and mix well. Pour the creamed butter/sugar/egg mixture into the blended fruits, nuts, and flour. Add the flavorings and the pumpkin pie spice, and stir all gently with a wooden spoon. Put in a heavy frying pan and bake at 375° for 30 minutes, stirring every 10 minutes. Pack in parchment-lined loaf pan and bake for 15-20 minutes at 375°.

When you make this cake, you are upholding a great tradition of our ancestors. Every homemaker should experiment with a fruit cake, and this is one that you can do!

Super Easy Coconut Cake, Family Style

Bring to boil in saucepan a mixture of <u>2 cups sugar, 1 cup milk, and 6 ounces frozen coconut</u>. Set aside. Make a 1-2-3-4 cake and pour half of the batter into prepared muffin tins. If you fill the cups half full, you can make 18 perfect cake muffins for the family to enjoy before the cake is ready. Bake your muffins in a 350° degree oven for 15-20 minutes, or until risen and lightly browned.

While you cook and cool your muffins, pour the remaining batter into a prepared 13 X 9 X 2 baking pan and bake at 350° for about 30 minutes. (Be sure the center is done by a finger-test: touch gently; if the cake does not show a print of your finger, it is done!) While cake is warm, pour on the warm icing. Insert knife in about 6 places to allow mixture to penetrate. Cover with foil and cool one hour.

Spread a small container of Cool Whip over the cooled cake and sprinkle with ½ of another package of coconut. Cover and refrigerate for an hour before serving.

This coconut cake is quite good and will do well for a family Sunday dinner. However, it is by no means to be compared to Miss Helen's famous five-layer coconut cake. At Christmas, you will want to make one of these!

Helen's Coconut Cake

Fluffy White Icing for a 5-layer Coconut Cake

2 cups sugar	4 beaten egg whites
2/3 cup water	½ cup 4X sugar
4 T white Karo syrup	2 t vanilla

<u>Mix</u> the sugar, water, and Karo in a heavy sauce pan. Stir and boil until mixture reaches 232° on a candy thermometer.

<u>Have ready</u> the beaten egg whites in the large bowl of your electric mixer.
<u>Without turning off mixer</u>, allow egg whites to beat at medium speed.
<u>Pour syrup gradually</u> into beating egg whites. Add the 4 X sugar and vanilla. <u>Beat</u> until the mixture will stand in peaks.

Take one large bag of Baker's Angel Flake Coconut and chop in food processor until as fine as you like. Spread icing on each layer, and sprinkle generously with coconut, gradually building cake. Frost the sides and top, and sprinkle coconut over all. Miss Helen can decorate the entire cake without making a big mess!

When Miss Ann makes a coconut layer cake, she uses a 7 Minute Frosting instead of the Fluffy White Icing recipe. Both icings work well. However, if you make 7-minute frosting, please do not attempt to construct a double boiler from two pots. Once Miss Helen did so, and the top boiler, because the metal expanded from the heat, suddenly blew to the ceiling, sending 7 Minute Frosting everywhere. Miss Helen escaped without permanent injury.

Seven Minute Frosting

Small Recipe	Large Recipe
2 egg whites	4 egg whites
¾ cup sugar	1 ½ cups sugar
1/3 cup white corn syrup	2/3 cup white corn syrup
2 T water	4 T water
¼ t cream of tartar	½ t cream of tartar
¼ t salt	½ t salt
1 t vanilla	1 ½ t vanilla

Combine all ingredients in the top of a double boiler. Cook over boiling water, beating constantly with an electric hand beater, for seven minutes, or until the icing will hold a peak. Remove from heat and continue to beat with electric mixer until the mixture is ideal to spread on cake. Frost each layer, top, and sides, sprinkling with coconut, and watch your layers rise.. It will stand tall and proud!

Nell Skinner's Chocolate Cake Filling

4 cups sugar
1 cup cocoa

1 1/3 cups evaporated milk
2 sticks butter
2 t vanilla

Step One: In a good sized saucepan with a strong handle, mix cocoa and sugar. Add milk and stir.

Step Two: Put the cocoa/milk/sugar mix on the stove, stirring constantly, until mixture comes to a full boil, and then boil and stir for 4 minutes.

Step Three: Remove pan from fire, add butter and vanilla, and pour chocolate mix into the bowl of an electric mixer. Leave unstirred for 15 minutes.

Step Four: Beat mixture in electric mixer until creamy.

Step Five: Use about half of chocolate mixture between layers of your cake.

Step Six: Place remaining icing in refrigerator. (The filling will still be soft.)

Step Seven: After the cake is stacked, with filling between layers, allow it to cool.

Step Eight: Retrieve the second batch of icing from the refrigerator, and beat and beat until fluffy and thick. Cover sides and top of cake. If you can't manage, call Miss Helen for counsel and advice.

Miss Helen's Quick Caramel Icing

2 lbs of light brown sugar
1 cup of carnation milk
2 sticks butter

4 cups powdered sugar
2 t vanilla

Mix together the sugar, milk, and butter in a heavy saucepan. Bring to a boil. Remove from heat, and pour over the 4 cups of powdered sugar in the big bowl of your electric mixer. Beat until smooth. Add vanilla. This icing will frost a 5 layer cake. You may sprinkle pecans on the top if desired.

Ann's Caramel Icing, from Mrs. S. R. Dull

1/3 cup sugar
1/3 cup water
1 ½ cups sweet milk
4 ½ cups sugar

¾ cup butter
¼ t soda
1 ½ t vanilla

Burn 1/3 cup sugar in large saucepan until melted and darkened. Add water (It will smoke up a storm!), and blend until there are no lumps. Add the milk, sugar, butter, and soda. Bring to a boil, stirring continually. Cook until the bubbling icing will leave a trace of the spoon. Remove from heat and beat until thick enough to spread on cake. (Energy and patience are required.)

Italian Cream Cake

1 cup Crisco
2 cups sugar
5 egg yolks
2 cups White Lily self-rising flour
1 t baking soda

1 cup buttermilk
1 t vanilla
1 cup coconut
1 cup pecans
5 egg whites

Cream sugar and Crisco until light and fluffy. Add egg yolks and beat at medium speed of electric mixer to blend. Sift baking soda into flour. Add flour alternately with buttermilk until batter is smooth. Stir in vanilla, coconut (which has been further chopped in a food processor), and pecans, which have been finely chopped. Fold in stiffly-beaten egg whites. Divide batter into prepared pans, and make four or five layers. Bake at 350° for 20 minutes or so, or until nicely browned and the cake begins to leave the edge of the pan.

Italian Cream Icing

1 stick butter

2 -8 oz packages cream cheese

2 pounds 10 X sugar

2 t vanilla

Beat butter and cream cheese in electric mixer until well blended. Add sugar and vanilla. Continue to beat until creamy. Spread on the layers of the cake and around sides and on top.

Red Velvet Cake

Red velvet cake is a dessert that our grandparents knew nothing about. However, I remember hearing about it in the early days of my marriage, in 1953. Unlike many "new" cake recipes, it is no longer a fad, and has earned its place as a classic.

2 ¼ cups sugar

3 eggs

2 ¼ cups oil

1 ½ t vinegar

1 ½ t vanilla

3 T red food coloring

3 ¾ cups self-rising flour

1 ½ t cocoa

1 ½ t soda

1 ½ cups buttermilk

In large bowl of electric mixer, beat eggs and sugar until fluffy. Add oil, vanilla, vinegar, and food coloring to the sugar and egg mixture. Combine the dry ingredients and add them alternately with the buttermilk. Blend all until silky and smooth. Bake in five layers at 350°. (See next page for Icing recipe)

Red Velvet Cake Icing

1 stick butter

2 -8 oz packages cream cheese

1 cup chopped pecans

2 pounds 10 X sugar

2 t vanilla

Beat butter and cream cheese in electric mixer until well blended. Add sugar and vanilla. Continue to beat until creamy. Add the chopped nuts. Spread between the layers of the cake and around sides and on top. *This one is Helen's favorite!*

Buttermilk Pound Cake

½ cup butter

½ cup Crisco

2 ¾ cups sugar

5 eggs

3 cups all purpose flour

½ t soda

1 cup buttermilk

½ t each, lemon & vanilla

Beat butter and Crisco in electric mixer until soft and smooth. Gradually add sugar, and beat thoroughly, until light and fluffy. Add eggs, one at a time, beating well after each. Sift flour with soda, and add to creamed mixture alternately with buttermilk. Stir in flavorings. Pour into prepared tube pan, and bake for 1 hour at 350°. Cool ten minutes and remove from pan.

This recipe will also make a sheet cake or two standard loaf cakes.

Mocha Cake

2/3 cup shortening
2 cups sugar
3 eggs, separated
1 square chocolate
½ cup hot coffee

½ cup milk
3 cups plain flour
3 t baking powder
½ t salt
1 t vanilla

Cream shortening and sugar well, and add egg yolks. When well mixed, add milk and chocolate, which has been dissolved in coffee. Add flour (sifted with baking powder and salt) and vanilla. Then fold in beaten egg whites. Bake at 350° in three 9 inch cake pans.

Busy Day Cocoa Icing

4 T boiling water
¼ cup butter
2 t vanilla

½ cup Hershey's Cocoa
2 cups 4x powdered sugar
2 T strong, hot coffee

Add boiling water to butter. Add vanilla, coffee, and cocoa. Beat until well blended, and add sugar. Beat until smooth and creamy, adding additional liquid, if necessary, until at right consistency to spread. Delicious on the Mocha cake, a warm sheet cake, brownies, or cupcakes. (This is a good, inexpensive, and quick chocolate icing with dark chocolate color. It keeps well for several days without hardening.)

Aunt Christine's Cream Cheese Pound Cake

3 cups sugar

3 sticks butter

1-8 oz package cream cheese

6 eggs

3 cups Swans Down cake flour

1 t each lemon and vanilla

Cream butter and cream cheese until smoothly blended. Gradually add sugar, and beat thoroughly, until light and fluffy. Add eggs one at a time. Add the flour, vanilla, and lemon. Pour into greased and floured tube pan, and bake at 325° for about 1 ¼ to 1 ½ hours.

Aunt Mae's Angel Food Cake

1 ¼ cups sifted Swans Down cake flour

½ cup sugar

1 ½ cups egg whites at room temperature

¼ t salt

1 ¼ t cream of tartar

2 t vanilla

1 1/3 cups sifted sugar

Combine the cake flour and the half cup of sugar and sift together four times. Combine egg whites, salt, cream of tartar, and vanilla in mixer. Beat until very soft peaks begin to form, and then add the 1 1/3 cups sifted sugar in four different additions. Beat further until the mixture will hold a firm peak but is not dry. With a whisk or spatula, fold the flour/sugar mixture into the beaten whites in four gentle additions. Pour into a 10 inch tube pan, <u>ungreased</u>. (It is best for you to set aside one pan to be used only for your angel food cake.) Bake at 375° for 35 minutes. Turn upside down for one hour, or until completely cool.

Aunt Mae Burch McCranie made the best angel food cakes in town, and many friends and relatives can remember enjoying this treat on a birthday.

Almond Pound Cake

½ pound butter
6 eggs
3 cups sugar

3 ¼ cups flour
1 t almond extract
½ pint whipping cream

Cream butter and sugar. Add eggs, one at a time. Add flour alternately with whipping cream, a small amount at a time. Mix well. Pour in tube pan. Put in cold oven and turn to 300°. Bake at 300° for 1½ hours. Delicious flavor!

Pineapple Upside Down Cake

<u>Use a large iron skillet, and have the following ingredients ready</u>:

4 T butter (half a stick)
1 cup brown sugar
1 No 2 can drained pineapple slices
10-12 drained maraschino cherries, whole

Melt the butter in the skillet. Add brown sugar and blend thoroughly. Spread evenly over the bottom of the pan. Arrange pineapple slices over the surface of this mixture, placing a cherry in the center of each slice of pineapple.

<u>Prepare the following batter</u>:

1/2 cup Crisco or butter
1 cup sugar
½ cup milk

1½ cups flour (self rising)
2 eggs

Cream shortening and sugar; add eggs, and add flour alternately with liquid. Pour the batter over the sugar and pineapple mixture. Bake at 350° for about 30 minutes. While hot, turn upside down on platter. Serve warm or cold with whipped cream.

Gingerbread

3 cups all-purpose flour	½ cup butter
1 t baking soda	1 cup light brown sugar
¼ t salt	2 eggs, well beaten
2 t each cinnamon and ginger	1 cup molasses
1 t cloves	¼ cup boiling water
¼ t nutmeg	1 cup buttermilk

Sift the flour, baking soda, salt, and spices together and blend thoroughly. Set aside. Cream butter and gradually add sugar, creaming until fluffy. Add eggs, beating well. Add a mixture of molasses and boiling water gradually, mixing well. Alternately add dry ingredients and buttermilk, starting and ending with dry ingredients, beating only until smooth. Turn batter into well-greased (bottom only) 13x9x2 inch baking pan. Bake at 350º about 35 minutes or until gingerbread tests done. Serve with lemon sauce.

Lemon Sauce

1 cup sugar	4 T butter
2 T corn starch	3 T lemon juice
2 cups boiling water	¼ t salt

Mix sugar and cornstarch together. Add the water gradually, stirring constantly. Boil for 5 minutes. Remove from fire and add butter, lemon juice, and salt. Serve on any kind of plain cake or on gingerbread.

Lemon Chess Pie

1 stick butter, softened

2 cups sugar

1 T cornstarch

4 eggs

3 lemons, juice & rind

In electric mixer, whip butter until soft. Add sugar, which has been sifted with corn starch; beat; add eggs, blending in each one. Add the lemon juice and rind, whipping gently. Pour into an unbaked pie shell and bake at 350° for 45 minutes.

Cherry Pound Cake

1 cup butter, softened

½ cup Crisco

3 cups sugar

6 large eggs

1 jar red (maraschino) cherries

½ t almond extract

½ t vanilla extract

3 ¾ cups plain flour

¼ t salt

¾ cup milk

Beat butter and Crisco with electric mixer until smooth and creamy. Gradually add the sugar, beating 5 to 7 minutes. Add eggs, one at a time, beating until yellow disappears. Stir in cherries, which have been drained and chopped. Sift together the flour and salt. Add to the butter mixture alternately with milk, beginning and ending with flour. Mix at low speed just until blended after each addition. Pour this prepared batter into greased and floured tube pan. Bake at 300° for about an hour and a half, or until a wooden toothpick inserted near the center comes out clean. (Turn page for frosting recipe)

Pineapple Cake Filling

Put all in a big sauce pan and cook over high heat. Continue cooking, stirring constantly, until mixture is thick. Cool and spread on cake.

1 large can crushed pineapple
3 cups sugar combined with 2 T corn starch

1 small can evaporated milk
1 stick butter

Cream Cheese Frosting

1-8 oz package cream cheese, softened
½ cup butter, softened

1-16 oz bag powdered sugar
1 t vanilla

Combine cream cheese and butter, blending until smooth. Add sugar and vanilla. Beat until light and fluffy. Spread on cool Cherry Pound Cake.

Lemon Pudding

2 eggs, separated
1 cup sugar
4 T butter

3 T lemon juice
2 T flour
1 cup milk

Beat egg whites until stiff. Cream butter and sugar. Beat yolks, and blend into butter/sugar mix. Into this, add the flour, juice of lemon, and milk. Fold in beaten egg whites. Pour into a casserole dish and bake in a pan of water at 325°, until meringue-top is lightly browned, and the custard has begun to set. Takes approximately 30 minutes.

Baked Custard

4 cups milk, slightly warmed　　　1 cup sugar
5 eggs　　　1 ½ t vanilla

Warm the milk. In separate bowl, beat eggs well and add sugar gradually. Add the warmed milk and vanilla, whisk, and pour into custard cups. Put cups in a baking pan of water, which comes up to 1½ inches on cups. Put pan in 350° degree oven. Lower to 325° if custard seems to be cooking too fast. The custard will require about 30 minutes baking time, if the milk has been warmed. It should set around edge, but tremble gently in center.

Boiled Custard

4 cups milk　　　4 eggs
1 cup sugar　　　1 t vanilla
2 t flour

Heat milk in top of double boiler. In a small mixing bowl, stir flour into sugar. In another bowl, beat eggs. Add the sugar mixture to eggs and beat well. Pour some of the hot milk into the egg, mixture and pour all back into the boiler. Cook, stirring constantly, until mixture coats the spoon. Do not bring to a boil. Mixture will be about as thick as buttermilk, but will thicken a little more when it cools.

Use this custard for banana pudding or for custard ice cream. If you use as an ice cream base, add 1 can condensed milk, 1 can evaporated milk, and 1 cup whipping cream, then churn until set.

Pecan Pie

½ cup butter

1 cup sugar

3 eggs, slightly beaten

¾ cup dark & light corn syrup, mixed

¼ t salt

1 t vanilla

1 cup chopped pecans

Cream butter, add sugar, and cream until light and fluffy. Add other ingredients and blend well. Pour in unbaked pastry shell and bake on lower rack at 375° for about 40 minutes. Do not overcook!

Butterscotch Pie

1 cup sugar

4 T butter

1 ½ c milk, warmed

Pinch of baking soda

5 eggs, separated

4 T corn starch

¼ cup cold water

1 t vanilla

8 T sugar (for meringue)

½ t cream of tartar

Cook and stir sugar until caramelized. Add butter. Stir warm milk into the sugar/butter mix. Add soda and simmer until all caramel is melted. Beat egg yolks. Pour part of the hot mixture into yolks, blend, and pour back into pot. Dissolve cornstarch in ¼ cup water. Add to hot mixture, and cook, stirring constantly, until thick. Add vanilla. To make meringue, beat whites and cream of tartar until foamy, then gradually add sugar, beating until mixture will stand in peaks. Fold a part of the fluff into your pie filling. Put into baked pie shell and cover with meringue. Bake at 325° degrees until meringue is lightly brown.

Butterscotch pie was the first new dessert that my mother made after her marriage. She bought a cookbook, and for years she cooked something new every day. From the very first, when Carlos got up from the table, he said, "Honey, that was de-lish!"

Graham Surprise Pie

Crust

2 T sugar, optional. 4 T butter, 1 package graham crackers rolled fine, 1 T half and half. Mix all ingredients and pat firmly with palm of hand to bottom and side of 10 inch pie pan, greased. Reserve ¼ of crumbs to sprinkle on pie.

Filling

1 can condensed milk	3 egg yolks
Juice of 3 lemons, rind of 1 lemon	3 egg whites

Mix all ingredients except egg whites. Then fold in stiffly beaten whites. Place filling in graham pie shell. Sprinkle with ¼ cup crust mix. Bake in moderate oven (350°) for 35 minutes or until filling sets and begins to crack.

Ice Box Cookies

½ pound butter	1 t baking powder
1 cup brown sugar	½ cup pecans, finely chopped
1 egg	½ t vanilla
3 cups plain flour, sifted with baking powder	

Mix ingredients in order. Knead like dough. Roll and wrap in wax paper. Put in freezer until ready to use. Slice thin and bake at 350° until done.

Tea Cakes

1 stick butter, unsalted
½ cup Crisco
2 cups sugar
3 eggs

½ cup buttermilk
1 t vanilla
4 or more cups self-rising flour

Using electric mixer, cream butter, shortening, and sugar. Add vanilla and eggs. Add flour to creamed mixture, alternating with milk. (Start with 4 cups of flour and add more if necessary.) Divide dough into rounds, wrap each in wax paper, then press flat. Freeze. The frozen dough is easy to handle, and you may bake a few cookies at a time. When ready to bake, roll the frozen dough until ¼ inch thick, cut out, then put on ungreased cookie sheet. Bake at 350° -375° for 15 minutes.

Pecan Tassies

<u>Crust</u>: 4 oz cream cheese, softened
½ cup butter
1 cup plain flour

In electric mixer, blend cream cheese and butter. Blend in flour. Chill dough before handling. Pinch off pieces of dough and press into miniature muffin pans.

<u>Filling</u>: 1 egg
¾ cup brown sugar
1 T butter, softened

1 t vanilla, dash of salt
¼ cup finely chopped pecans
24 whole pecans (optional)

Beat together egg, brown sugar, and butter. Add vanilla and salt. Beat until smooth. In each muffin cavity sprinkle some pecan chips on crust. Add egg mixture and top with a pecan half, if desired. Bake at 325° for 25 minutes or until filling is set. Cool before removing from pans.

Date Dreams

¼ t salt
3 egg whites
1 ¾ cups 10 X sugar mixed with 1 T flour
2 cups chopped pecans
1 cup chopped dates
1 t vanilla

Add salt to egg whites and beat to a stiff foam. Add sugar sifted with flour, one tablespoon at a time. Continue beating until stiff. Fold in nuts, dates, and vanilla. Drop with a spoon on parchment-lined bake sheet. Cook at 300° for 30 minutes.

Nutty Fingers

7/8 cup butter
4 T of 10 X sugar
2 cups flour
1 t warm water
2 t vanilla
1 cup minced nuts

Cream butter and sugar. Blend in other ingredients. Chill until firm enough to shape between fingers. Form into small date-shaped pieces. Bake at 400° for 10-12 minutes. Roll at once in sifted powdered sugar.

Cracker Pie

4 egg whites
1 cup sugar
½ t baking powder
1 t vanilla
½ cup chopped pecans
14 Ritz crackers, rolled fine
½ pint whipped cream

Beat egg whites until stiff. Add sugar, baking powder, and vanilla, and continue beating until blended. Roll Ritz crackers until very fine and gently fold into egg white mixture. Fold in pecans and pour into 9 inch greased pie plate. Bake at 350° for 25-30 minutes. When cool, slice as pie, top with whipped cream, and sprinkle more chopped nuts on top.

Bread Pudding

6 slices day old bread
3 T butter
½ cup raisins
¼ t salt

¾ cup sugar
3 eggs, beaten
3 cups scalded milk
¼ t cinnamon

Toast bread and spread with butter while hot. Arrange toast in buttered baking dish 10 X 6 X 2. Sprinkle with raisins. Stir salt and all but 2 T sugar into beaten eggs. Add milk and blend. Pour over toast and let stand 10 minutes. Press toast firmly down into milk so that toast soaks up most of liquid. Mix cinnamon with remaining 2 T sugar and sprinkle over top. Bake at 350° for about 25 minutes or until a knife inserted comes out clean and top is touched with brown. Serve warm or cold.

Condensed Milk Lemon Pie

<u>Mix</u>:

    1 can Eagle Brand sweetened condensed milk   Grated rind of 2 lemons
    1/2 cup lemon juice   4 egg yolks

<u>Beat</u>:

    Four egg whites and 8 T sugar until stiff meringue forms.

<u>Fold</u>:

    Some of the meringue mixture into the pie filling.

<u>Spoon filling into a baked pie crust</u> or a prepared graham cracker crust. Top with meringue and bake at 325° until meringue turns golden brown.

Lemon Pie

5 eggs, separated	1 ½ cups sugar
1 ½ cups milk	Grated rind of 1 lemon
4 T corn starch	Juice of 2 lemons
1 T butter	(10 T sugar for meringue)

Mix all ingredients except egg whites, and cook, stirring constantly, until thick. Set aside. Beat whites and add the 10 T sugar gradually, and beat until stiff peaks form. Fold ¼ of the whites into pie mixture, pour into baked crust. Use remaining whites for meringue. Bake at 325° until brown.

Lemon Fluff Pie

5 eggs, separated	3 T water
¼ cup lemon juice	1 cup sugar
Grated rind 1 lemon	

Prepare a pie shell as instructed in pastry section. Cook as directed and set aside.

Separate eggs. Beat yolks in top of double boiler until thick. Add lemon juice and rind, the water, and half the sugar. Cook over boiling water, stirring until thick. Remove from water. Beat whites until fluffy, add remaining sugar and continue beating into a firm, fine meringue. Fold half the meringue into the warm yolk and lemon mixture, and when evenly blended, heap into pie shell, top with remaining meringue mixture, and bake at 325° until lightly browned.

Austin's Favorite Apple Pie

8 tart apples, Granny Smith or McIntosh	1 t cinnamon
2 cups sugar	1 stick butter

Line a deep-dish Pyrex pie plate with pastry. (See recipe in bread/pastry section.) Prebake the crust slightly, but take from the oven before it browns completely. Peel, core, and slice the apples. Place the apples in the pastry. Mix the cinnamon and sugar and pour over the apples. Melt butter and pour over all. Roll out the top crust in a circle, and cut into strips for a lattice top. Bake at 350° for about 45 minutes, or until nicely browned.

This pie is delicious served with sharp cheddar cheese or with Breyers or homemade ice cream.

Coconut Cream Pie

Pinch of salt	1 t vanilla
¾ cup sugar	1 cup coconut
¼ cup flour	10 T sugar for meringue
1 ¾ cups milk	¼ t cream of tartar
5 eggs, separated	

Mix salt, sugar, and flour in large saucepan. Add milk, beaten egg yolks, and vanilla. Mix well, and cook until thick. Add coconut. (You may use fresh, frozen, or one cup of Baker's Angel Flake, cut into smaller morsels in the food processor.) Place egg whites in large mixing bowl, and whip until they become frothy. Add sugar gradually, and continue beating until stiff peaks form. Scoop out ¼ of the meringue and fold into coconut filling. Pour the coconut mixture into the prepared and baked pie shell. Top with remaining meringue. Bake at 325° until the meringue is nicely browned.

Chocolate Cream Pie

1 cup sugar	5 eggs, separated
3 T flour	1 T butter
3 T cocoa	1 t vanilla
1 ½ cups milk	2 T sugar for each egg white

Make a pastry as described in pastry/bread section. Freeze. When read to bake, take your pie shell from the freezer, and prick with a kitchen fork. Cook at 400° until lightly browned.

For filling, mix sugar, flour, and cocoa in large saucepan. Add milk, vanilla, and beaten egg yolks. Cook until thick and add butter. Set aside. Have egg whites at room temperature. Add ¼ t Cream of Tartar. Beat at high speed of electric mixer, and when the whites begin to froth, start to add the sugar gradually. Beat until the meringue will hold a stiff peak. Add 1/4 of this meringue to chocolate mixture, and fold in. Pour into pie shell. Scoop remaining meringue over top, and bake in 325° degree oven until lightly browned.

Egg Custard Pie

5 eggs	1 ½ cups milk
1 cup sugar	1 t vanilla
1 T corn starch or 2 scant Ts flour	

Beat eggs well and add the sugar, which has been mixed thoroughly with the flour or cornstarch. Add the milk and vanilla and mix well. Strain this mixture into an unbaked pie crust. Bake at 350° until set. Do not overbake

Raisin Pie

4 eggs, separated
½ cup sugar
¼ cup melted butter

½ cup white Karo syrup
1 cup raisins
8 T sugar

Beat egg yolks well, and add sugar, butter, and syrup. Stir in raisins. Pour into an unbaked pie shell. Bake pie for 30 minutes at 350°, or until set. Make meringue by beating egg whites with ¼ t cream of tartar. When whites are frothy, begin to add sugar slowly. Continue to beat until stiff peaks form. Pour over the warm pie. Return to oven and bake at 325° until meringue is brown.

Helen's Disappearing Apple Tarts

Cook 8 oz of dried apples in a small amount of water until soft.

Drain in a colander. Turn apples into bowl and mash well.

Add 1 cup sugar, stir, and place in refrigerator.

Make biscuit dough, using 2 cups of flour. (See recipe in bread section.)

Leave dough in bowl for several hours, beating down from time to time.

Turn dough out on floured cloth, and knead until smooth.

Roll out with rolling pen to about ¼ inch thickness.

Cut out rounds with a two-inch biscuit cutter.

Reroll left-over dough and repeat.

With a rolling pen, roll each dough-round into a circle the size of a saucer.

Place a heaping tablespoon of apples in center of each.

Fold over, and press edges lightly together with fingers.

Trim each pie by going around rough edge with a saucer, and you will have a half-moon shape.

Heat oil to 375° in electric skillet with deep sides. You should have the oil 1½ inches deep. Gently place each tart in the hot grease. Do not overlap. When tarts rise to the top, take a dinner fork and prick three or four times around the tart edges. Turn. When both sides are brown, remove and drain on paper towels.

When these tarts appear at a family reunion, they will not last until the end of the line.

Chocolate Delight

1 stack pack graham crackers, crushed	2 cups Cool Whip, divided
1-6oz pkgs instant chocolate pudding	¼ cup butter
1- 8 oz pack of cream cheese	3 cups milk
1 cup powdered sugar	½ cup chopped pecans

Mix the graham crackers with the half stick of butter. Press into a flat Pyrex dish that has been sprayed with Pam. Bake in an oven at 325° until set, but not too brown. Remove from oven and cool. Beat the package of cream cheese with the powdered sugar, and fold in one cup of the Cool Whip, and spread over the graham cracker crust. Prepare the two packages (4 oz each) instant chocolate pudding with three cups of milk, not four. Spread the chocolate mixture over the cream cheese layer. Top the chocolate with another cup of Cool Whip. Sprinkle pecans over the top. If you want a superb dessert, use Chocolate Cornstarch Pudding (below) instead of the instant.

Chocolate Cornstarch Pudding

3 squares Hershey's baking chocolate	¼ t salt
3 cups rich milk (whole milk)	1 T butter
1 cup granulated sugar	1 t vanilla
¼ cup cornstarch	

Melt baking chocolate in double boiler over simmering water. When chocolate is melted, add milk. Stir until well blended. Combine the sugar, cornstarch, and salt, and add a small amount of hot chocolate mixture, stirring vigorously. Return all to the double boiler and cook until thickened, stirring constantly. Cook 15 minutes longer. Add butter and vanilla. Spoon into serving dishes and press waxed paper directly on to surface of pudding. Cool and chill. Serve with sweetened whipped cream. (Recipe from the *Hershey's 1934 Cookbook*)

Aunt Evelyn's White Caramel Icing

3 cups sugar

1 ½ cups milk

1 stick butter

1 t vanilla

Put all together in heavy boiler, and cook over high heat until boiling. Continue cooking until the mixture will form a coating on the spoon, about 8-10 minutes. Remove from fire and beat until smooth and thick enough to spread on cake. This icing will fill and frost a four or five layer 1-2-3-4 cake.

Demon Cake

4 squares Hershey's baking chocolate

1 cup butter (2 sticks)

2 ½ cups granulated sugar

1 ½ cups buttermilk

3 cups sifted cake flour

1 t baking soda

½ t baking powder

½ t salt

5 eggs, separated

1 t vanilla

Melt the chocolate in a double boiler over simmering water. Cream the butter and sugar, and add the melted chocolate. Sift together the flour, soda, baking powder, and salt, and add to the cake batter alternately with the buttermilk. Beat the egg yolks well and blend. Beat the egg whites until stiff, and fold into the cake batter.

Add vanilla. Pour into four greased and floured cake pans. Bake at 350° for 30 to 35 minutes. Top with Seven Minute Frosting.

This cake is beautiful for a birthday.

Can't Stop Cookies

These cookies are a favorite with all of Helen's relatives, church members, and friends. You know what happens when you eat one—you can't stop!

2 sticks butter	½ t soda
1 cup sugar	1 t vanilla
1 ½ cups all purpose flour	½ cup chopped nuts
½ t baking powder	2 cups Rice Krispies

Cream butter and sugar. Add vanilla. Mix flour, baking powder, and soda, and add slowly to sugar mixture. Add nuts. Fold in Rice Krispies. Drop by teaspoon or small scoop on to parchment-lined baking pan. Bake at 350° for 8-10 minutes.

Ambrosia

My father always believed this dessert to be the food of the gods. Ambrosia is the wonder of all foods—good to eat and good for you.

Peel plenty of oranges, removing all white spots. Cut out orange sections. As you finish cutting the sections from each orange, squeeze out remaining juice. Keep peeling until you have a huge bowl of orange sections. Add as much coconut as you like. My mother always used one fresh, grated coconut. Sprinkle generously with sugar, sweetening the fruit to your taste, and toss all together. Chill. Serve with your holiday cakes.

Hot Fudge Pudding Cake

1 cup self rising flour

2 T cocoa powder

½ cup milk

1 t vanilla flavoring

2/3 cup sugar

2 T butter, melted

1 cup chopped pecans

Mix together flour, sugar, and cocoa. Add melted butter, milk, and vanilla, Mix well. Fold in nuts. Pour into buttered 2 quart flat casserole dish.

Mix together:

1 cup packed brown sugar, 4 T cocoa powder

Sprinkle over mixture in dish. Pour 1 ¾ cups boiling water over all and DO NOT STIR. Bake at 350° degrees for 30 minutes. Serve with vanilla ice cream.

New Orleans Brownies

These brownies were once the featured item at a family bakery in New Orleans. Jean Carrie, granddaughter of the bakery's founders, gave the recipe to Don when she was at Wofford College. Since then, they have become a favorite with family and friends. Rich, rich, and delicious!

1 pound butter at room temperature

4 cups sugar

8 eggs

2 cups all purpose flour

1 t salt

1 cup cocoa

2 cups chopped nuts

1 t vanilla flavoring

Cream butter and sugar until light and fluffy. Add eggs, one at a time. Sift together the flour, salt, and cocoa. Add these dry ingredients gradually, and beat until the entire brownie mixture looks glossy. Add nuts and vanilla. Blend.

Bake in two 9X3X 13 pans, which have been greased and floured, or use one large restaurant size pan. Bake at 300° for one hour.

Cousin Sarah's Fudge Bar Cake

One of our Burch relatives moved away from Dodge County and established a newspaper in Greer, S.C. For a long time, we never saw them. Then, in 1955, Don and I moved to Spartanburg, near Greer. My mother called Sarah and Ed Burch and made <u>sure</u> we all got together. What a blessing! For the next forty years, our families shared recipes and Sundays and holidays. Time and time again, Don and I and our children sat down to a special meal with Sarah and Ed and their sons. When we were the hosts, Cousin Sarah would come up the walk smiling. "I do love an occasion," she often said. She was a great cook! Here is one of her favorite recipes.

½ cup cocoa

½ cup Crisco

2 cups white sugar

½ cup buttermilk

1 cup hot water

2 cups self-rising flour, mixed with ½ t baking soda

Mix above ingredients until blended.

Add: 2 eggs   1 t vanilla

Mix well.

Pour into a greased 9x13 pan. Bake for 40 minutes at 350°.

Icing:

Beat 2 cups powdered sugar and 1 egg (or ¼ cup cream). Add one stick of softened butter and 2 squares bitter chocolate (melted). Add one teaspoon vanilla.

Spread over top of cake.

Peach Cobbler

1 quart peaches, canned or fresh	1 cup sugar
¾ cup sugar	1 cup self-rising flour
1 cup water	1 cup milk
1 stick butter	

If using canned peaches: Put peaches and juice in pot with ¾ cup sugar and 1 cup water. Bring to a boil. Let cool. If using fresh peaches, peel and slice, then add sugar as needed. Set aside. Put stick of butter in 9x13 Pyrex baking dish. Place in a 350° oven and melt. Mix 1 cup sugar, milk, and flour. Pour this batter over melted butter. Spoon peaches over batter. Gently pour juice over top. Do not stir. Bake at 350° for 30-35 minutes.

Steamed Lemon Pudding Cups

1 T butter, melted	Granulated sugar

Butter four 1-cup ramekins and coat with sugar.

2/3 cup granulated sugar	2 eggs, separated
2/3 cup buttermilk	2 T lemon juice
1 T lemon zest	¼ cup all-purpose flour
¼ t salt	

Mix together egg yolks, buttermilk, lemon juice and zest. Add flour, sugar and salt. Mix well. Beat egg whites until stiff and fold into lemon mixture. Divide among the four ramekins. Place in baking pan and add hot water half way up on the ramekins. Bake at 325° for about 30 minutes until top springs back when lightly touched.

Let cook and invert onto dessert plates, garnish with fresh blueberries, if desired, and sprinkle with powdered sugar. Delicious!

Bourbon Banana Pudding Cheesecake

2 cups finely crushed vanilla wafers, graham crackers, or ginger snaps
½ cup chopped pecans
½ cup unsalted butter, melted
3 large ripe bananas
1 T lemon juice
¼ cup light brown sugar
1 T bourbon whiskey or vanilla
4-8 oz packs cream cheese, softened
1 cup granulated sugar
4 large eggs
1 T bourbon whiskey or vanilla
½ cup roughly crushed vanilla wafers
1 cup heavy whipping cream
¼ cup powdered sugar
1 t bourbon whiskey or vanilla
1 banana, sliced (for garnish)

Preheat oven to 350°F. Grease a 9-inch springform pan and wrap the outside with aluminum foil. Set aside.

In a food processor, pulse the crumbs and pecans until they are finely chopped. While the processor is running, stream in the melted butter and pulse until the crumbs are moist and come together. Dump the crumbs into the prepared pan and pat down with your hands. Form the crust with the back of a spoon or a measuring cup, making sure to flatten out the bottom and bring the crumbs up the sides of the pan. Bake in preheated oven for 10 minutes. Remove and allow to cool completely.

In a small sauce pot, mash the bananas until they are completely mashed and smooth. Add the brown sugar and lemon juice. Cook over medium heat for a few minutes until the sugar has melted and the bananas cook slightly. Remove from heat and add the bourbon or vanilla if using. Mix and allow to cool down completely.

In the bowl of an electric mixer, fitted with the paddle attachment, whip the cream cheese for 2 minutes, until light and fluffy. Slowly stream in the granulated sugar and continue to cream together for another 2 minutes. Add the eggs one at a time, mixing well after each addition. Add in the bourbon or vanilla extract if using. Scrape down the sides and bottom of the bowl, mix again. Stir in the banana mixture until just incorporated. Spread the filling over the crust and place in a roasting pan. Pour hot water into the larger roasting pan going half way up the springform pan. Bake in a 350°F oven for about 45 minutes to 1 hour. It may depend on your oven. You'll know the cheesecake is done when the center is firm and doesn't jiggle when shaken. If you find that the cheesecake is browning rapidly before being done, lower the oven slightly. Once done, place on a cooling rack and allow to cool down completely. Place in the fridge and chill for at least 8 hours.

In a large bowl add the cold heavy whipping cream. Beat until the cream begins to thicken. Add the powdered sugar and bourbon or vanilla extract if using. Continue to beat until the cream forms soft peaks. Cut the cheesecake into slices and pipe whipped cream onto each slice. Top with a vanilla wafer cookie and a banana slice. Sprinkle the middle of the cheesecake with the crushed vanilla wafers. Serve right away. Store any leftovers in the fridge covered with plastic wrap. Will keep for up to 5 days. Enjoy!!

As the years have passed, Helen's grandchildren have stayed close by, most of them living right here in Dodge County. Ann's grandchildren, on the other hand, have scattered across the country. Her oldest grandchild, Caroline Moore, is living in Raleigh, North Carolina. It seems far away. Still, we share the great moments, which almost always include food. Recently, Caroline baked this beautiful cheesecake for her boyfriend, Ben Watts. On the same occasion, she decorated her porch with twinkling crystal lights, set a festive table, and invited a party of friends for his birthday dinner. The cheesecake itself made the whole occasion unforgettable. Caroline got the recipe from *The Candid Appetite*. It only took four hours to concoct the whole thing! Love is grand!

Church Dinners

Be present at our table, Lord;
Be here and everywhere adored;
Thy creatures bless and grant that we
May feast in Paradise with Thee.

John Cennick, 1741 (Tune: Old Hundredth)

The church dinner is an old custom in the South, and all Southern ladies have made their contributions to this tradition. Although the trend today is to enjoy the church dinner inside in air-conditioned comfort, many of us remember attending "dinner-on-the-ground" at camp meetings or revivals.

Helen and her mother, my Aunt Evelyn, have long lists of heavenly credits for "feeding the preacher" and preparing church dinners during the summer revival seasons. For these good deeds, I hope that they will find many stars in their crowns.

These days, Helen and I continue to cook and bake for church occasions. Helen's church, Sand Grove Baptist, is in the country that I so loved to visit as a child. Although my church in Spartanburg, South Carolina, never required my services as a cook, I find that the First Presbyterian Church of Eastman has frequent need of my offerings, and I am glad to serve with the other women of my congregation.

Many fine recipes for church culinary fare are included in this cookbook. Check the index for the following:

Pot Roast	Biscuits and Rolls
Fried Chicken	Salads
Vegetable Casseroles	Apple and Cream Pies
Main Dish Casseroles	Layer Cakes

Southern Corn Bread Dressing

1 cup finely chopped celery	4 cups crumbled cornbread
1 cup finely chopped onion	2 cups dry crumbled white bread
½ cup butter	A little salt and pepper
One quart chicken stock	3 or 4 eggs, well beaten

Note: None of the people in my family care for sage in their dressing, but we were surprised once when, on demand, we added fresh sage to our recipe. The flavor from fresh sage is nothing like the dried herb. If you wish to experiment, add a little. You won't be disappointed.

In microwave bowl, cover celery and onions in a little water, add the butter and microwave about three minutes, until the vegetables are a bit softened in texture but still crisp. You may sauté vegetables in a saucepan if you prefer. Dry out the bread slices in a slow oven before crumbling, if necessary. In a very large bowl, mix the chicken stock with the crumbled breads, raw eggs, and all other ingredients. Blend well. You may need to add more stock. The dressing should be soft, the consistency of cake batter or a thick milkshake. That is the secret! The dressing will dry as it cooks. Preheat oven to 425°. Bake in greased baking dish (13 X 9) for about 40 minutes. Spoon out. Serves 10-12.

Every good cook in our family makes a fine dressing to serve with the Christmas turkey. This recipe will make you famous! Serve dressing with roast pork, baked ham, baked chicken or even roast beef. When you add dressing to the menu, your guests know they are special.

Betty Harrington

Betty Harrington has been cooking at the Presbyterian Church for longer than any woman in the congregation, and she remembers wonderful dinners from many years ago. She also grows her own vegetables, and one of our favorite treats at church is something cooked fresh from her garden.

Betty Harrington's Fresh Green Beans

2 cups water
2 t ham seasoning (Goya)
1 t salt
1 t sugar
2 T canola oil
1 quart green beans

Pick beans when they are very young and slim and tender. Wash them at least three times, and break them into 2 inch pieces or leave whole—your choice. Put water and seasonings on the stove. Bring to a boil, and then add the beans. Return to a boil, cover, and cook gently until tender, about 30 minutes. If needed, you may add a little more water as the beans cook.

Miss Betty's White Acre Peas

1 quart fresh peas
2 T vegetable or canola oil
1 t salt
2 cubes chicken bouillon
1 t sugar
2 cups water

Shell and wash peas at least two times. Put water and seasonings on the stove and bring to a boil. Add peas to the pot and cover, and cook at medium heat until they are tender and done, approximately 45 minutes. Multiply this recipe 2 or 3 times for a church dinner.

Corn Southern Style

You may have your own recipe for corn, but this is how Miss Betty does it!

1 pint of corn, cut off the cob	Pepper to taste
1/3 cup dry milk	1/3 cup cooking oil
2 T sugar	1 cup of water
1 t salt	2 T flour

Wash corn and cut from cob. Mix powdered milk, sugar, salt, pepper, and oil in a large, heavy saucepan.   Pour the corn into this mixture. Blend the flour smoothly into the cup of water and add to corn mixture. Cook on a slow to medium temperature, stirring frequently to prevent the corn from sticking. Cooking time will be from 15 to 20 minutes.

Mary Graham

Mary Graham also keeps a vegetable garden, and she often brings a big pot of black-eyed peas to a church dinner. She doesn't stop there! Her fresh carrots, just pulled from the earth, and her potatoes and onions from the garden make a pot roast irresistible.

If you don't have a vegetable garden, you may still cook something special to accompany the meat course. Try stewed tomatoes or fresh corn, and you won't have any leftovers to bring home!

Stewed Tomatoes

Stir ¾ cup of sugar into 2 cans of tomatoes, and allow to simmer until quite thick and deepened in color. If still too thin when you are ready to serve, thicken with 1 T flour mixed with 2 T water. Good with pork roast, butterbeans, or white acre peas. The tomatoes will keep in the refrigerator for a week or more, so you can make these ahead if you wish.

Candied Yams

Peel 5 pounds sweet potatoes, slice, and put into a heavy pot on top of stove. Add ½ cup water. Add plenty of sugar—about a cup and a half for a good pot of potatoes. Add a half stick of butter. Do not cover. Simmer slowly for an hour, or until you have a nice, thick syrup on sweet potatoes that are glazed and firm.

Southern Cornbread

An excellent accompaniment to fresh vegetables is a big pan of cornbread! Try the recipe below.

1 1/2 cups corn meal	1/2 cup all purpose flour
1 t baking soda	1/2 t salt
1 1/2 cups buttermilk	1/3 cup melted shortening
1 egg, beaten	

Place all ingredients into a mixing bowl and stir to blend. Pour into a greased iron skillet, a muffin pan, or corn stick pans. Bake at 400° for 20 minutes or until brown. (An iron skillet takes longer, usually about 30 minutes at 400°.)

Gravy for Chicken and Roast

It is a good idea to bring gravy to your church dinner, for gravy can be heated at the last minute to accompany the fried chicken or to pour over the pot roast.

Milk Gravy: Reserve 4 T bacon drippings. Stir in 4 T flour. Slowly add 2 cups milk and 1 cup water, stirring until thickened. Thin with a little more liquid if necessary. (Make chicken gravy the same way, using drippings from the fried chicken.) Although gravy is delicious on hot biscuits, this item is not on the American Heart Association Diet.

Roast Beef Gravy: Whisk 3 T flour into ¼ cup water until smooth and blended. Pour this blend into roast beef juices from a pot roast. Blend thoroughly and cook, stirring constantly, until mixture is thick and smooth. (You should start with at least 3 cups of beef broth from the roast.)

Chicken a la King

Many people have never tasted Chicken a la King, but Mrs. E. M. Harrington, Sr., had a great recipe. Try it at your next women's meeting!

½ cup chopped mushrooms	4 T butter, with 4 T flour
½ cup chopped green pepper	3 ½ cups milk
½ cup chopped celery	3 chicken breasts, chopped
2 T butter	1-8 oz pack cream cheese

In a saucepan, saute mushrooms, green peppers, and celery in 2 tablespoons of butter. Set aside. In large, heavy pot, melt 4 T butter. Add 4 T flour and blend. Gradually add the milk to make a white sauce, stirring until nicely thickened. To this mixture add the mushrooms, peppers, and celery. Stir in the chopped chicken breasts. (Use a whole chicken, if you prefer, using the best of the dark meat along with the chicken breasts.) Grate cold cream cheese, and stir gently into mixture. When the sauce is smooth and hot, serve on crisp biscuits or in pastry shells. (A variety of pastries are available in the freezer at the super market.)

24 Hour Salad

Mrs. Z. K. Foster, grandmother of Zandra Smith and Joni Moore, often brought this special salad to church dinners, and everybody wanted seconds!

2 eggs beaten	1 cup whipped cream
4 T vinegar	2 cups Royal Anne cherries
4 T sugar	2 cups diced oranges
2 T butter	2 cups miniature marshmallows

Cook the eggs, vinegar, and sugar, stirring constantly until they are thick and creamy. Remove from the heat, add butter, and let cool. When the mix is cold, fold in the cream, the fruits, and the marshmallows. Place in the refrigerator (do not freeze) and let stand 24 hours before serving. Stir several times as it chills.

There is a rumor around church circles that men don't like tomato aspic. Surely this cannot be true! An aspic is a cool and palatable addition to a featured main course like chicken a la king, and it is wonderful with seafood.

Marilyn Spradley's Spicy Tomato Aspic

2 ½ envelopes unflavored gelatin	¾ cup chopped green pepper
1-3 ounce box lemon Jello, + ¼ t salt	¾ cup chopped celery
3 cups V8 juice, divided	¾ block cream cheese, cold
1 T grated onion	1/3 cup green olives, stuffed

Sprinkle gelatins over one cup V 8 juice and allow to stand one minute. Cook over medium heat, stirring until gelatin dissolves. Stir in onion, salt, and remaining 2 cups of juice. Chill until the consistency of unbeaten egg whites. Fold in the pepper and celery. Spray a 9 X 13 X 2 inch Pyrex pan or gelatin mold with Pam. Cut cream cheese into miniature pieces (about the size of a large pea), and toss into pan. Chop olives and sprinkle these among the cheese pieces. Pour tomato mixture over all. Chill until congealed. Turn out when ready to serve.

One Pot Shrimp Creole for a Church Luncheon

Marilyn says that the recipe below is Ethel's creation and one the family much enjoyed. Ethel was a "second mother" to the growing Spradleys.

1 cup regular rice, uncooked	2 T fresh lemon juice
2 cups uncooked shrimp, clean and deveined	1 t salt
2 T Wesson oil	¼ t pepper
1 15 ounce can Hunt's tomato sauce	2 cups hot water

Cook rice in skillet in oil until golden. Add remaining ingredients. Cover and simmer for 30-35 minutes, or until rice is done.

Connie McDaniel's Creamed Potatoes

I have known few people in my life who did not long for a big bowl of creamed potatoes to accompany steak, fried chicken, roast, meat loaf, or roast pork. Genuine creamed potatoes are a smash at a church dinner!

5 pounds potatoes	½ to ¾ cup milk
Salt to taste	½ pint sour cream
1 stick butter	Additional salt and pepper

Peel and slice the potatoes, and put in a big heavy saucepan with 2 cups salted water. Cover, bring to a boil, and cook until tender. Pour off the water and place the potatoes in large bowl of electric mixer. Add butter (cut up), milk (a little at a time), sour cream, and salt and pepper to taste. Whip until creamy and smooth. You may wish to melt the butter and heat the milk.

Macaroni and Cheese

The foods we bring to church dinners have changed over the years, but some dishes endure the test of time. Since depression days, everyone expects to find the comfort of a macaroni and cheese among the offerings. **Here's how you do it!**

Pour two cups of elbow macaroni into a large pot of boiling water, with 1 tablespoon of salt. While the macaroni cooks, make a cream sauce: In a heavy pot, melt ½ stick butter, add 4 T. flour, and blend. Add 3 cups of milk gradually, and stir constantly until thick. Drain the macaroni in a colander, then pour this into the sauce. Add at least two cups of cheese, more if you like! Blend. Pour all into a greased casserole, and top with more cheese. Bake at 350°, just until bubbling nicely around the edges. Yum!

Lasagna

<u>Step I</u>: The Sauce

2 pounds lean ground beef	1 t salt
1 small can tomato paste	½ t pepper
1 large can crushed tomatoes	1 T oregano
1 cup onions, chopped	1 T basil
1 cup celery, chopped	2 bay leaves
1 T sugar	2 jars of pasta sauce

Brown the ground beef, pour off drippings, and add all other ingredients. Choose the very best pasta sauce, one with mushrooms but without meat. Stir everything together until the sauce is blended and bubbling, and then cut down the heat and allow to simmer for at least two hours.

<u>Step II</u>:

1 package lasagna noodles	3 eggs
2 pints ricotta cheese	16 oz mozzarella cheese
1 jar parmesan cheese	

Cook lasagna noodles until they are flexible and tender. This takes about 10-12 minutes, usually. (Follow the directions on the package, but put some oil in the water so that noodles will not stick together.) While these cook, blend together two pints of ricotta cheese, 1 cup grated Parmesan, and three eggs. Drain the noodles, and put a layer of these noodles in a long Pyrex pan sprayed with Pam. Cover the noodles with a layer of the sauce. Add 8 ounces of mozzarella cheese, then cover with half the ricotta mixture.

Repeat. For final layer, spread noodles over all, cover heavily with sauce, and sprinkle generously with the parmesan. Bake at 350° for 30-40 minutes, until bubbling around the edge and piping hot. This dish will stay hot all the way through Sunday School and services, and will be ready when the church family gathers to dine.

Rae Spradley's Quick Banana Pudding

The secret of this wonderful pudding is in the presentation. Rae chooses a beautiful pedestal bowl, of clear crystal. The pudding sparkles from top to bottom and makes a gorgeous display on the dessert table.

If you want to bring a lovely dish to church, and don't have the time to do something that is extremely time-consuming, try Rae's pudding.

2 packages instant vanilla pudding mix	1 cup half and half
2 cups milk	1 cup sour cream

Whisk above ingredients gently together and set aside.

(You will also need <u>bananas</u>, <u>vanilla wafers</u>, and a pint of <u>whipping cream</u>.)

In the serving bowl, put a layer of <u>vanilla wafers</u>, top with <u>bananas</u>, and repeat until bowl is 2/3 filled. Pour pudding over all. Top with whipping cream. Keep in cool place (not refrigerator) until ready to serve.

Sand Grove Baptist Church

At Sand Grove Baptist Church, all the women in the congregation are excellent cooks. Helen testifies that every family brings to each dinner a generous and well-stocked picnic basket. When all the foods are arranged, tables are groaning with barbecue and Brunswick stew, fried chicken, chicken and dumplings, baked chicken, baked ham, fresh peas and beans, butterbeans, corn, squash, and macaroni and cheese. On another table, you will find sliced tomatoes, cucumbers, pasta salad, potato salad, broccoli salad, and many congealed salads. Among such a gracious plenty, it is very hard to choose.

The choice becomes more difficult when you see the table of tempting and luscious desserts. Among the favorites are Helen's apple tarts, chocolate and lemon pies, and 12-layer chocolate cake. (Over the last twenty months, Helen has baked 109 pound cakes, 50 chocolate cakes, 36 coconut cakes, 39 Italian Creams, 14 caramel cakes, and 39 red velvet cakes.)

Brenda Watkins is a beloved cook among the Sand Grove experts, and she is the one who always does the barbecue and Brunswick stew. She, too, is known among the congregation for her special-occasion layer cakes. For every birthday and wedding celebration, she creates a masterpiece. Miss Brenda's offerings feature a delicious buttercream icing and elaborate decorations. With a church as old as Sand Grove Baptist, there are many occasions to celebrate and a great deal of history to appreciate.

Sand Grove Baptist is 100 years old, with a cherished and respected past. In the early days, a great deal was expected of the congregation. The Articles of Personal Conduct, written in 1932, outlined a strict code:

1. It is the duty of each member to attend each regular meeting.
2. Anyone dealing in "hardened spirits" shall be dealt with.
3. Any member engaged in dancing, or in playing any instrument for dance, shall be dealt with.
4. Any member who gets intoxicated will be expelled upon the second offense.

Although there are complete records of offenses and punishments, nothing is ever written in the church history about how many times the women of this church and every church in every county in Georgia brought food for the long revival services, how many times they churned ice cream, how many times they shared whatever they had with their neighbors. But it doesn't really matter that they did not record these sacred things. Whether we are in town or country, in cities or small communities, these memories are written on our hearts.

Ann and Helen

Many times on July 4, I visited with Helen and her family and ate barbecue and Brunswick stew. This delicious feast would be on trestle tables in the front yard (swept clean for the occasion) and there was a gracious plenty for all—neighbors, field hands, relatives, and strangers. Tin tubs of various sizes were filled to the top, and cakes of every variety were alongside. The tables were loaded with goodness. The old fashioned Brunswick stew served on this occasion required long hours of preparation. Today, try this one! This great recipe, given to the Inn by Charmon McKinney, is the best you can imagine, not only for the Fourth of July, but for a cold autumn day. It is also great if you are going camping. Keep the supplies on the pantry shelf at all times if you habitually expect the unexpected guest.

Brunswick Stew

2 cans chicken broth
1 pound ground beef, browned and drained
1 large onion diced
2 medium potatoes, diced
2 cans barbecue pork (or 2 cups freshly made)
2 small cans mixed chicken (cut up), or 1 large, or you may use a deli chicken
2 cans whole kernel corn, yellow
1 can creamed corn
1 can diced tomatoes
2 cans English peas, drained, or one package frozen butterbeans
1 can tomato sauce
1 small bottle Heinz catsup
Hot sauce to taste
3 beef bouillon cubes and 2 to 3 cups water (Add water as it cooks, if needed.)
Salt and pepper to taste

Mix together, and cook all day in a crock pot. If you cook on the stove, simmer at least one hour.

The "Amen"

The "Amen" to a recipe book should certainly be a dessert, the innocent sin of all church folk. In this spot, we pay homage to a dessert that is a joy to bring to the table: a homemade cheesecake. Cheesecakes are fun to make, deeply appreciated, and lovely to look at. This one is Helen's favorite!

Cheesecake

Crust

1 ½ cups graham cracker crumbs   ¼ cup sugar
¼ cup melted butter

Mix the above ingredients together and place in 9 inch springform pan. Cover bottom and 1 inch on the sides. Bake 10 minutes at 350 and cool.

Filling

3-8oz packages cream cheese   4 eggs
1 ½ cups sugar   2 t vanilla

Topping

2 cups sour cream   ½ cup sugar
1 t vanilla

In electric mixer, beat cream cheese and sugar until smooth. Add eggs, one at a time, beating until blended. Add vanilla. Pour this mixture into crust. Bake 50 minutes at 350°, until light gold and puffy. Cool 15 minutes on wire rack. Mix topping ingredients together, and spread over cheesecake. Bake at 450° for 10 minutes. Cool completely and refrigerate. When ready to serve, remove sides from springform pan. Slice into pie-shaped wedges. You may use cherry or blueberry topping, if you wish, and fresh strawberries in season.

Post Script (P. S.)

By definition, a postscript (P.S.) is an addendum to a letter after the letter itself has been composed and signed. In this fifth edition of *A Gracious Plenty,* we have surely written the composition and finished the course. How could we have more to say about good food and good cooking, or about what Andy Griffith once called "gracious living"?

Perhaps it is time, before we say goodbye, to remind ourselves of habits and attitudes closely associated with the food we eat. For one thing, we must remember that food in a sack from a fast food restaurant is not a meal, and the back seat of the car is not a dining room table. The food may taste good, and the children may be laughing and singing, and that's a fine memory. But this ride in the car is not a substitute for sitting around the family table. The table may be a place to study, a place to pile books or DVD's, or a place to wrap Christmas presents. That's fine. Yet we must not forget that the table is a place for people, young and old, to draw together and to share joys, stories, news, and food. The setting need not be elaborate, but it does require an effort. For instance, at Helen's house, the young cousins once set up a coffee table for six, with cushions for chairs, and a centerpiece of leaves and wild flowers. The food was delicious, and the table setting lovely. The conversation was lively and the memory permanent.

If we, like our mothers and grandmothers, are truly homemakers, it is essential that we give our families an opportunity to interact. It is also true that the father figure in our homes must help to make the evening meal an *occasion*. In a *Leave-It-to-Beaver* household, somewhere in never-never-land, there is a kitchen table for the morning, and a dining room properly set for the evening. There are candles on the dining room table on special days, and there are always flowers.

At the Dodge Hill Inn, we start the day with a special and wonderful breakfast, our guests gathered 'round. And whatever happens, we have Sunday dinner, and we fight to keep it going. Conscientious homemakers consider it a duty to serve and be served, and this sense of duty stays with us all our lives.

Our duty done brings the blessing of good food, lovingly prepared. We believe that this gracious plenty, heaped up over and over again, gives us long and productive lives. May we appreciate this earthly life, enjoy many a feast, and thank God for all good things.

Ladies and gentlemen, keep the faith.

Ann, Helen, and Terri

About the Authors

Ann Hemperley Dobbs was born and raised in East Point, Georgia, but she spent her childhood summers in Eastman, where her mother's people live. "Miss Ann" married H. Donald Dobbs in 1953, and she graduated from Agnes Scott College in 1955. In the fall of '55, Ann and her husband moved to Spartanburg, SC, where Professor Dobbs joined the faculty of Wofford College, a position he held for forty years. Ann began her own teaching career at The Spartanburg Day School in 1970, and taught there for 25 years. As a teacher of English, she was an avid supporter of the arts and of the drama department at SDS. She wrote the play *Mount Vernon Ladies*, which was performed at Mt. Vernon, the home of George Washington, in 1992. Ann now lives in Eastman, and she and her cousin Helen Hardin Peterson run the Dodge Hill Inn. Miss Ann is a loyal member of the First Presbyterian Church in Eastman and serves on the Session. She has nine grandchildren, and plenty of room for them to visit! She loves to have guests and to give a party, and everyone in her family has a copy of the new fifth edition of *A Gracious Plenty*.

Helen Hardin Peterson grew up in Dodge County, and except for her college years, has lived here all her life. She graduated from Georgia Southwestern in 1955. Her mother and father, always hospitable, lived on their farm in the beautiful countryside near Milan, Georgia. The family served the community through their service to Sand Grove Baptist Church, where Helen is still a faithful member. "Miss Helen" and her husband Pete had 38 years together. Helen has always been a good business woman, as she proved during the ten years that she ran and managed *Pa Pete's*, the family's popular restaurant in Milan. Helen not only managed and served, but made all the desserts and did all the baking for the restaurant. She is a prolific reader and orders inspirational romances by the dozen, reading two or more books a day. Since she moved into town, Helen has started a thriving homemade-cake business to take up the slack in her schedule. If she is not at the Inn, you will find her in her kitchen making one of her gorgeous cakes. All fourteen of her grandchildren are welcome anytime!

Index

Beverages

Ann's Favorite Punch	37
Chilled Herbal Cooler	20
Cranberry Banana Frappe	20
Helen's Favorite Punch	38
Hot Chocolate	21
Mocha Punch	39
Russian Tea	36
Slush	21
Sox Hemperley's Famous Egg Nog	39

Breads

Angel Yeast Waffles	61
Aunt Christine's Apple Walnut Muffins	59
Banana Nut Bread	57
Biscuits, Angel	50
Biscuits, Cheddar Garlic	54
Biscuits, Riz	53
Biscuits, Southern Cream	53
Cherry Nut Bread	56
Cranberry Nut Bread	55
Date Nut Bread	56
Giant Popovers	54
New Orleans Beignets	60
Pancakes, Buttermilk Light	60
Pie Pastry I	58
Pie Pastry II	59
Pumpkin Bread	58
Rolls, Easy	51
Rolls, Ice Box	52
Rolls, Quick	51
Rolls	52
Sour Cream Gems	50
Strawberry Nut Bread	57
Sweet Potato Bread	55

(See also breakfast foods)

Breakfast Foods

Apple Dumplings	19
Apple Sauce Muffins	9
Apricot Coffee Cake	18
Baked Apples	14

Biscuits, Plain	5

Breakfast Foods

Biscuits, Cinnamon	5
Biscuits, Orange	10
Boiled Custard	15
Breakfast Cup	19
Blueberry Muffins	9
Butterscotch Rolls	16
Caramel French Toast	6
Cheese Soufflé	11
Coffee Crumb Cake	17
Cream Cheese Danish	16
Crepes	8
Egg Tortillas	5
Favorite Breakfast Casserole	7
Fried Potato Patties	19
French Toast Puff	4
Fresh Fruit	15
Fried Apples	14
Fruit Bowl	15
Grits	12
Grits Casserole	12
Ham and Eggs ala Swiss	10
Hot Spiced Fruit	13
King and Prince Oatmeal Raisin Muffins	18
Pancakes	3
Parmesan Potatoes	13
Quiche	11
Scrambled Eggs	12
Tomato and Basil Frittata	6
Waffles	3

Casseroles, Soups, and Main Dishes

Barbecue Pork Chops	84
Beach Shrimp	94
Beef Stroganoff	85
Boiled Shrimp	90
Chicken Casserole	81
Chicken and Dumplings	82
Chicken Enchiladas	93
Chicken Pot Pie	92
Chicken Salad Casserole	81
Chicken with Sour Cream and Bacon	82
Cranberry Chicken	86
Crock Pot 3 Cheese Tortellini with Spinach	95
Deviled Crab	91
Dinner in a Dish	82
Down Home Meatloaf	92
Easy Baked Chicken	86
Easy Chicken Pie	94
Family Baked Chicken	89

Fried Chicken	87
Gumbo	84
Miracle Pasta	95
Party Beef Dinner	85
Plum Sauce, Aunt Mae's	92
Scalloped Oysters	83
Shrimp Casserole	90
Shrimp Casserole w/Green Noodles	90
Shrimp Creole	91
Soup, Cream of Broccoli	80
Soup, Cream of Tomato	80
Soup, Potato	79
Standing Rib Roast	88
Stuffed Shrimp	89
Sunday Pot Roast	88
Sunday Roast Beef	84
Zesty Gold Corn Chili	93

Cookies, etc.

Apple Tarts, Helen's	131
Can't Stop Cookies	134
Date Dreams	125
Ice Box Cookies	123
New Orleans Brownies	135
Nutty Fingers	125
Pecan Tassies	124
Tea Cakes	124

Desserts for the Family

Ambrosia	134
Baked Custard	121
Boiled Custard	121
Bourbon Banana Pudding Cheesecake	138
Bread Pudding	126
Chocolate Pudding	132
Chocolate Delight	132
Gingerbread	118
Lemon Pudding	120
Lemon Sauce	118
Peach Cobbler	137
Steamed Lemon Pudding Cups	137

Cakes

Almond Pound Cake	117
Aunt Mae's Angel Food Cake	116
Buttermilk Pound Cake	114
Aunt Christine's	

Cream Cheese Pound Cake	116
Cherry Pound Cake	119
Coconut Cake, Easy	108
Coconut Cake, Helen's	109
Cousin Sarah's Fudge Bar Cake	136
Demon Cake	133
Hot Fudge Pudding Cake	135
Italian Cream Cake	112
Mocha Cake	115
1-2-3-4 Cake	106
Pineapple Upside Down	117
Red Velvet Cake	113
Stir Fruit Cake	108

Frostings and Icings

Busy Day Cocoa Icing	115
Butter Cream Icing	107
Caramel, Ann's (from Mrs. Dull)	112
Caramel, Helen's Quick	111
Chocolate Cake Filling	111
Cream Cheese Frosting	120
Fluffy White Icing	109
Italian Cream Icing	113
Lemon Cheese Cake Filling	107
Pineapple Cake Filling	120
Red Velvet Cake Icing	114
Seven Minute Frosting	110
White Caramel-Aunt Evelyn	133

Pies

Austin's Apple Pie	128
Butterscotch Pie	122
Chocolate Cream Pie	129
Coconut Cream Pie	128
Condensed Milk Lemon Pie	126
Cracker Pie	125
Egg Custard Pie	129
Graham Surprise Pie	123
Lemon Chess	119
Lemon Fluff Pie	127
Lemon Pie	127
Pecan Pie	122
Raisin Pie	130

Party Foods

Cheese Delights	28
Cocktail Meatballs	30
Corn Dog Muffins	33
Crab Dip	24

Crab Meat Balls	24
Dill Toast Points	32
Fudge	35
Helen's Divinity	35
Peanut Butter Strips	31
Pecan & Cream Cheese Stuffed Dates	27
Pecan Pie Muffins	34
Raw Vegetable Dip	27
Sardine Puffs	29
Sausage Phyllo Cups	33
Shrimp in Bacon	25
Shrimp Dip	25
Shrimp Mold	25
Smoked Salmon Cheesecake	31
Spinach Dip I	26
Spinach Dip II	26
Stuffed Mushrooms	27
Toasted Pecans	29
Toasted Cheese Canapés	28
Tortilla Roll Ups	34

Sandwiches

Cheese & Tomato Sandwich	45
Chicken Salad	43
Cream Cheese Onion Spread	44
Cucumber Sandwiches	47
Date Nut Sandwich Filling	46
Egg Salad	43
Ham and Cheese Rolls	44
Ham Salad	43
Party Sandwich Loaf	43
Pimento Cheese	46
Pineapple Sandwiches	47
Scones and Cream	45

Salads

Asparagus Salad	66
Broccoli Salad	64
Broccoli Cauliflower Salad	66
Buttermilk Lime Salad	73
Coca-Cola Salad	71
Cole Slaw	74
Cranberry Salad, Easy	72
Cranberry Salad, Simple	71
Cucumber Ring	68
Cucumber Salad	67
Dorito Salad	77
Frozen Fruit Salad, Easy	73
Grape Salad	75
Greek Shrimp Pasta Salad	76
Green Bean Salad	69

Layered Green Salad	63
Lettuce Wedge Salad	64
Lime Jello Salad	72
Pasta Salad	65
Perfection Salad	70
Pineapple Carrot Salad	71
Pork and Bean Salad	69
Potato Salad	70
Potato Salad, Debbie's	76
Shrimp Salad	67
Six Cup Salad	73
Strawberry Salad	72
Tomato Aspic	68
Waldorf Salad	74
Waldorf Salad Variation	75
Wild Rice and Cranberry	65

Vegetables

Aunt Miriam's Vegetable Casserole	102
Broccoli Casserole	99
Brown Rice	102
Cabbage Casserole	101
Fresh Corn Pudding	97
Fried Onions	100
Glazed Carrots	98
Horseradish Carrots	101
Spinach Soufflé	98
Squash Soufflé	97
Stuffed Tomatoes	100
Sweet Potato Soufflé	98
Tomato Pie	103
Vidalia Onion Pie	99

The Church Dinner

Banana Pudding	151
Brunswick Stew	154
Candied Yams	145
Cheesecake	155
Chicken a la King	147
Cornbread, Southern	146
Corn, Southern Style	144
Creamed Potatoes	149
Gravy, Milk	146
Gravy, Roast Beef	146
Green Beans	143
Lasagna	150
Macaroni & Cheese	149
Salad, 24 Hour	147
Shrimp Creole, One Pot	148
Southern Cornbread Dressing	142
Spicy Tomato Aspic	148
Tomatoes, Stewed	145
White Acre Peas	143

www.ingramcontent.com/pod-product-compliance
Lightning Source LLC
Chambersburg PA
CBHW050454110426
42743CB00017B/3356